JOURNAL OF LAW & CYBER WARFARE

FOREWORD
Cyber Warfare and the Corporate Environment
By Chris Colvin, Daniel Garrie, and Siddartha Rao

ARTICLES
Cyberwarfare: Attribution, Preemption, and National Self Defense.
By John Dever and James Dever

Cyber Redux: The Schmitt Analysis, Tallinn Manual and US Cyber Policy.
By James E. McGhee

Is Cyber Espionage a Form of Market Manipulation?
By Noah Bledstein

Volume 2 | Spring 2013 | Issue 1
(c) 2012 – 2013. Journal of Law & Cyber Warfare.
All Rights Reserved.

www.jlcw.org

EDITORS
Daniel B. Garrie, Esq., Editor-in-Chief
Siddartha Rao, Esq., Executive Editor

Associate Editors
Stephen Williams, Esq., Editor-at-Large

EDITORIAL BOARD

Alan Roper	Alex Carrillo
Chris Colvin	Dick Crowell
Douglas DePeppe	George Hull
Gus Dimitrelos	James Christiansen
Jeff Bardin	Jonathan E. Turner
Joseph E. Weiss	Larry Ponemon
Noah Bledstein	Patrick Grey
Richard Borden	Roei Haberman
Russell Walker	Thomas A. Johnson
Uma Chandrashekhar	William Spernow
Yoav Griver	

JOURNAL STAFF

Giri Vakkalanka	Kim Kopoff
Margaret Mak	Radhika Tiwari
Renee Almassizadeh	Sarah E. Haines

Foreword

Cyber Warfare and the Corporate Environment

By Chris Colvin*, Daniel B. Garrie**, and Siddartha Rao***

---

* Mr. Colvin has over 20 years of experience in the Intellectual Property field and is the co-founder of a leading IP law firm, Colvin Hudnell LLP. Mr. Colvin is also an experienced entrepreneur, having launched several successful companies, including the first and largest private social media networks for in-house attorneys (In The House), law firm partners (Partnero) and Ivy League alumni (IvyLife). Mr. Colvin has a Bachelor of Science degree in Aerospace Engineering from Princeton University and a law degree from George Washington University. Mr. Colvin can be reached at chris@colvinhudnell.com.

** Mr. Garrie has over 15 years of experience in cyber security, digital privacy, e-discovery, and Internet field and is the co-founder of a leading consulting firm, Law & Forensics LLC. Mr. Garrie is also a serial entrepreneur having built and sold several successful Internet and mobile startups and currently is a partner at Pulse Advisory, a venture development firm, and is on the Board of Advisors of several startups including Get.it, Treemo Labs, Equivio, and Eccentex. Mr. Garrie has served as an Electronically Stored Information Liaison, Forensic Neutral and Forensic Expert in state and federal court. Mr. Garrie has a Bachelor of Arts degree and Master of Arts degree from Brandeis University in Computer Science and a law degree from Rutgers School of law. Mr. Garrie can be reached at Daniel@lawandforensics.com

I. INTRODUCTION: THE "BACK DOOR" IS OPEN AND CYBER-TERRORISTS ARE IN OUR MIDST

As we inaugurate another issue, the Journal of Law and Cyber Warfare ("JLCW") takes the opportunity in this foreword to reflect on the recent developments in this area. We also present cyber-security data from hundreds of business entities across the world in a first-of-its-kind survey.

Prior to the terrorist attacks of September 2001, mass shootings at schools and universities, and other highly-publicized acts of domestic and international terrorism over the past two decades, the "front door" of corporations, government agencies, and educational institutions largely stood open. Most adults recall a time when any vehicle could pull up to the White House gates, and any person could walk into the headquarters of a Fortune 500 company, or through airplane security, with a water bottle and their shoes on. Sadly, but necessarily, that front door of physical security has closed.

While the front door has closed, the back door is wide open. The era of Big Data has fully arrived, and information assets of immense financial, public, and personal value are stored and regularly transmitted by

---

*** Mr. Rao is an Assistant General Counsel at Guidance Software, Inc. serving as a subject matter expert in cyber security, data privacy, and electronic discovery. Mr. Rao previously practiced at the law firm of Zeichner Ellman & Krause, LLP, specializing in complex commercial litigation, including anti-money laundering, insurance, bankruptcy, intellectual property, and electronic discovery strategy. Mr. Rao has a law degree from the University of Texas Law School of Law, where he was an associate editor for the Texas Law Review, and a Bachelor of Arts degree in Mathematics from Middlebury College. Mr. Rao can be reached at siddartha.rao@guidancesoftware.com. The thoughts expressed herein are solely the authors' own and not those of Guidance Software, Inc.

corporations, governments, and universities in a widely dispersed, hugely complex, and ever-changing labyrinth of computers, mobile devices, and telecommunications networks. Indeed, the current and future wealth and prosperity of developed nations rests largely on information assets rather than physical ones. Yet, as JLCW's Cyber Security Survey shows, there are shockingly few legal, regulatory, or private data-security standards and practices that have emerged to protect these enormously valuable assets, even as cybercrime has grown tremendously in sophistication and frequency. The back door is open and the cyber-terrorists are in our midst.

The editors of JLCW hope that this first-of-its-kind survey will serve as a wake-up call to corporate, government, and academic leaders around the world to roll up their sleeves and get to work securing that back door, an effort we believe is essential to our future collective security and prosperity.

II. CYBER WARFARE: A BURGEONING THREAT

State-sponsored hackers and non-state-affiliated collectives have launched cyber warfare on corporations and government entities, targeting information assets in their efforts to disrupt business and government operations.[1] With the rise of worldwide interconnectivity through massive information networks, we are well into the age of "Postmodern Terrorism."[2]

---

[1] Simonite, Tom, *Hacking Industrial Systems Turns Out to be Easy*, MIT Technology Review (August 1, 2013) (describing vulnerabilities in control systems used to manage energy infrastructure that are now connected to the internet), *available at*: http://www.technologyreview.com/news/517731/hacking-industrial-systems-turns-out-to-be-easy/.

[2] Laquer, *Postmodern Terrorism*, FOREIGN AFFAIRS 14 (Sept.-Oct. 1996) (describing a hypothetical cyber attack against the Federal Reserve's main switching terminal in Culpepper, Virginia and the dire consequences that could follow).

Cyber-war and cyber-crime events are increasing rapidly. Just earlier this year, the New York Times described multiple sophisticated hacking attempts on American banks. The hacker group calling itself Izz ad-Din al-Qassam Cyber Fighters claimed responsibility in online postings.[3] American officials suspect the group and its attacks originated from Iran. The scale of these attacks is chilling as they "showed a level of sophistication far beyond that of amateur hackers." One cyber security expert noted: "The scale, the scope and the effectiveness of these attacks have been unprecedented . . . ."[4]

In March of this year, American Express and JP Morgan Chase also found themselves the victims of sophisticated disruptive cyber-attacks that knocked both companies' systems offline.[5] In the same month, thirty-two thousand computers in the South Korean bank and television networks were incapacitated by a cyber-attack.[6]

As the incident rate and threat level of cyber attacks are on the rise, some governments are taking aggressive measures to manage these risks. For example, the Israel Defense Forces launched a cyber-defense control center in February of this year.[7]

---

[3] Perlroth and Hardy, *Bank Hacks Were Work of Iranians, Officials Say*, NEW YORK TIMES BI (January 9, 2013), *available at*: http://www.nytimes.com/2013/01/09/technology/online-banking-attacks-were-work-of-iran-us-officials-say.html?_r=0.
[4] *Id*.
[5] Perlroth and Sanger, *Cyberattacks Seem Meant to Destroy, Not Just Disrupt*, NEW YORK TIMES BI (March 29, 2013), *available at*: http://www.nytimes.com/2013/03/29/technology/corporate-cyberattackers-possibly-state-backed-now-seek-to-destroy-data.html.
[6] *Id*.
[7] Lappin, *IDF cyber-defense control center goes online*, THE JERUSALEM POST (February 13, 2013), *available at*: http://www.jpost.com/Defense/IDF-cyber-defense-control-center-goes-online.

III. LACK OF LEGAL AND REGULATORY NORMS

With a growing need for international cooperation on cyber defense, the last year has seen the publication of landmark treatises on international law and cyber conflict such as the 215-page "Tallinn Manual," published by the Cooperative Cyber Defense Center of Excellence.[8] Yet enforceable legal norms remain elusive, and a broadly-backed international convention on cybercrime and warfare has not materialized.[9]

Despite a consensus that the international law of armed conflict applies generally to cyber warfare, it is still unclear how far such application may extend or whether application is even possible where tracing attacks to responsible parties is not practicable. To this day, debate in cyber-warfare law continues on issues as fundamental as the definition of cyber warfare: e.g., does cyber warfare encompass any operation that targets civilians or only those where physical harm results, consistent with Protocol 1 to the Geneva Conventions?[10]

Attempts to bring cyber warfare within the purview of international-legal norms have been inconsistent. One example is the International Information Security Agreement (the "Security Agreement") ratified by the Shanghai Cooperation

---

[8] The Tallinn Manual is *available at*: https://www.ccdcoe.org/249.html.

[9] This issue's article *Cyber Redux: The Schmitt Analysis, Tallinn Manual and US Cyber Policy* by James E. McGhee considers the state of international norms in cyber warfare, with particular analysis of the Tallinn Manual and other attempts to create a general paradigm for response to cyber attacks.

[10] This issue's article *Cybersecurity: Covert Action and Clandestine Operations* by John and James Dever explores such definitional issues around cyber warfare and summarizes this scholarly and commentarial debate.

Organization (the "SCO").[11] The Security Agreement reflects antithetical interests of the SCO-ratifying nations as compared to the United States and Europe,[12] listing as major threats the "dominant position in the information space" of Western nations and the "dissemination of information harmful to the socio-political systems, spiritual, moral, and cultural environment of the [ratifying nations]."[13] The Security Agreement also explicitly affirms the SCO-ratifying nations' control over information technology and communications, including any speech considered "politically destabilizing."[14] As such, the Security Agreement represents not a consensus, but rather a divergence of interests between "Western" nations and other regimes.[15]

---

[11] The SCO member nations consist of China, Russia, Kyrgyzstan, Uzbekistan, Kazakhstan, and Tajikistan.

[12] This issue's article *Is Cyber Espionage a Form of Market Manipulation* by Noah Bledstein explores the competing interests of the Sinosphere and Western nations by posing the question of whether acts considered as cyber-attacks under the umbrella of cyber-warfare are more accurately understood as market manipulations subject to existing legal norms.

[13] Goldsmith, *Cybersecurity Treaties: A Skeptical View*, FUTURE CHALLENGES IN NATIONALSECURITY AND LAW, (ed. Berkowitz) (2011), *available at:* http://www.futurechallengesessays.com.

[14] Rosenzweig, Paul, CYBER WARFARE: HOW CONFLICTS IN CYBERSPACE ARE CHALLENGING AMERICA AND CHANGING THE WORLD at 207 (ABC-CLIO 2013); Abraham D. Sofaer, David Clark & Whitfield Diffie, *Cyber Security and International Agreements*, in PROCEEDINGS OF A WORKSHOP ON DETERRING CYBERATTACKS: INFORMING STRATEGIES AND DEVELOPING OPTIONS FOR U.S. POLICY 179, 186 (2010), *available at*: http://www.nap.edu/openbook.php?record_id=12997.

[15] Indeed some scholars have argued that the SCO is itself a pretext for pursuing autocratic political ends. *See e.g.*, Ambrosio, Thomas, *Catching the 'Shanghai Spirit:' How the Shanghai Cooperation Organisation Promotes Authoritarian Norms in Central Asia*, 60 EUROPE-ASIA STUDIES 8, 1321–44 (October 2008) (arguing that scholars have myopically focused on the democracy-promoting aspects of international organizations and failed to examine the

This conflict was starkly illustrated by a recent incident in which a group of Chinese hackers known as APT1 (accused of being affiliated with the Chinese army) were caught hacking into a decoy water control system for a US municipality.[16] This incident occurred less than two months after a meeting between President Obama and China's President Xi Jinping regarding, *inter alia*, cyber security issues.[17] Moreover, the United States itself has suffered a loss of credibility on issues of cyber security following the now-infamous revelations of the federal government's PRISM surveillance program, further complicating international dialogue on these issues.[18] These seemingly irreconcilable differences may derail any efforts to develop legal norms supported by supra-regional international consensus.[19]

IV. CYBER WARFARE, THE CORPORATE MARKET AND JLCW'S SURVEY RESULTS

In response to the uncertainty and risk in the cyber security environment, JLCW sought to gather data

---

potential for such organizations, for example the SCO, to promote autocratic regimes and concentrations of power).

[16] Simonite, Tom, *Chinese Hacking Team Caught Taking Over Decoy Water Plant*, MIT TECHNOLOGY REVIEW (August 2, 2013), *available at*: http://www.technologyreview.com/news/517786/chinese-hacking-team-caught-taking-over-decoy-water-plant/. The system was set up by Kyle Wilhoit, a researcher at security firm Trend Micro. Wilhoit "actually watched the attacker interface with the machine," and concluded it was "100 percent clear" the attack was intentional.

[17] Jeff Mason, et al. *Obama, China's Xi to Discuss Cyber Security in June Meeting*, REUTERS, (May 28, 2013) *available at*: http://www.reuters.com/article/2013/05/28/us-usa-china-hacking-idUSBRE94R02720130528.

[18] Carroll, Rory, *Barrack Obama and Xi Jinping Meet as Cyber-Scandals Swirl*, THE GUARDIAN (June 8, 2013), *available at*: http://www.theguardian.com/world/2013/jun/08/obama-xi-jinping-meet-cyberscandals.

[19] Goldsmith, *supra* n. 10.

on cyber security in the corporate market, conducting a comprehensive survey across business areas and countries. The survey addresses fundamental issues including cyber preparedness, threat response, and relationship of internal investigation and auditing to regulatory and government response mechanisms. JLCW received responses from nearly four hundred businesses across nearly eighty industries, ranging from small partnerships to large-multinational corporations.

These survey findings paint a stark and alarming picture of corporate cyber preparedness:
- Basic knowledge of information security systems, procedures, and protocols to deal with cyber threats is inconsistent and inadequate in many, if not most, industries.
- The lack of real incentives to report cyber breaches encourages a culture of silence, doing a disservice to regulators and harming targets of cyber crimes.
- "Big Data" – and the accompanying cyber security risks – is not limited to just a handful of industries, but is pervasive across nearly every business sector, from the arts to telecommunications to healthcare.

A. Survey Respondent Profile

Respondents to the JLCW Cyber Security Survey included organizations spanning a wide spectrum of sectors and types.

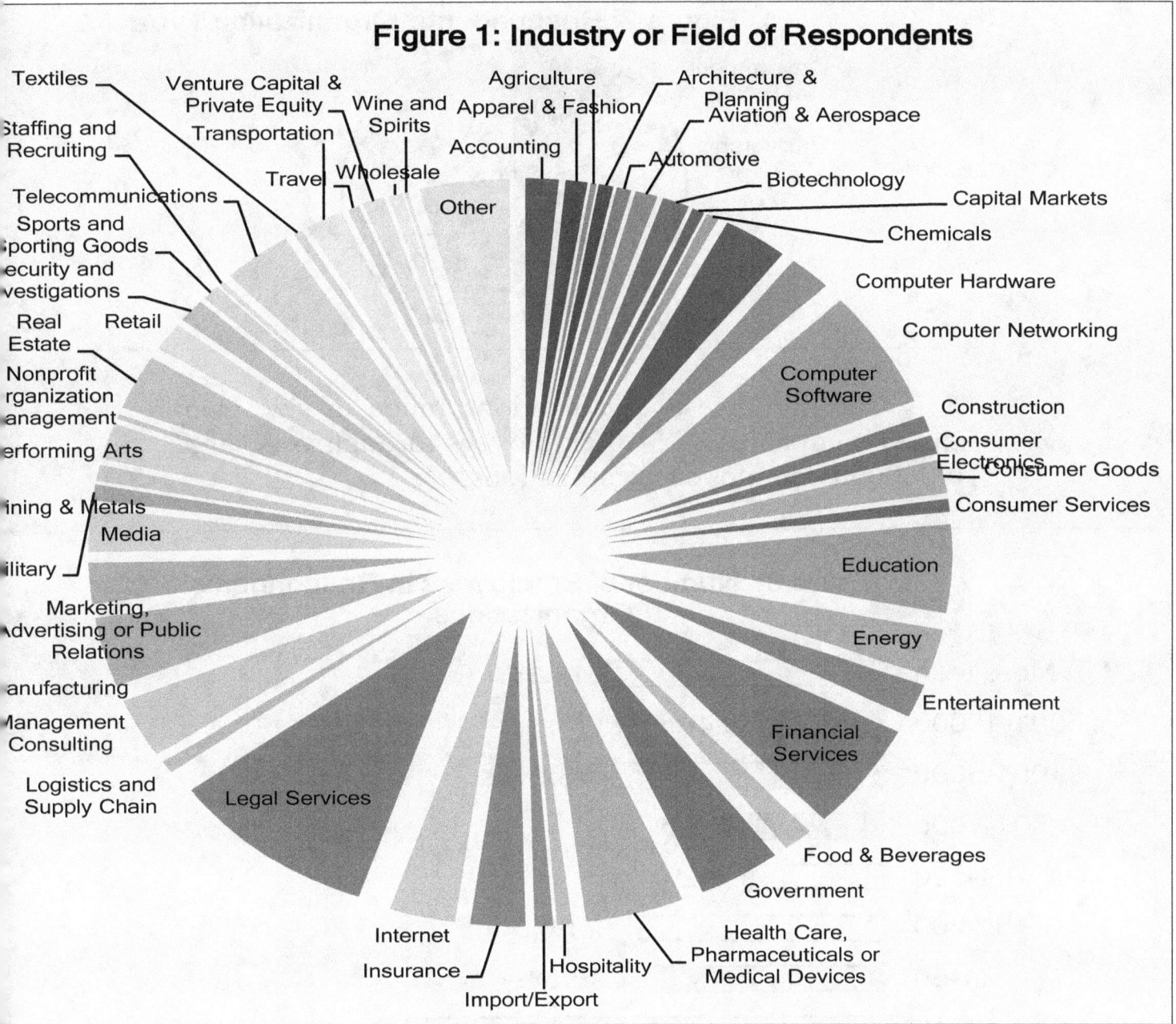

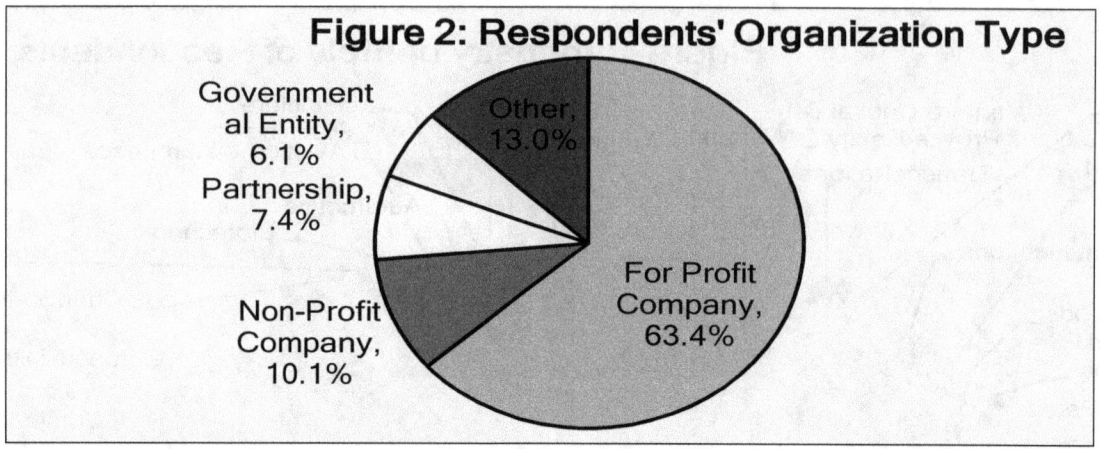

Further, these organizations range in size from smaller companies of 1-10 employees through very large 10,000 plus-employee organizations.

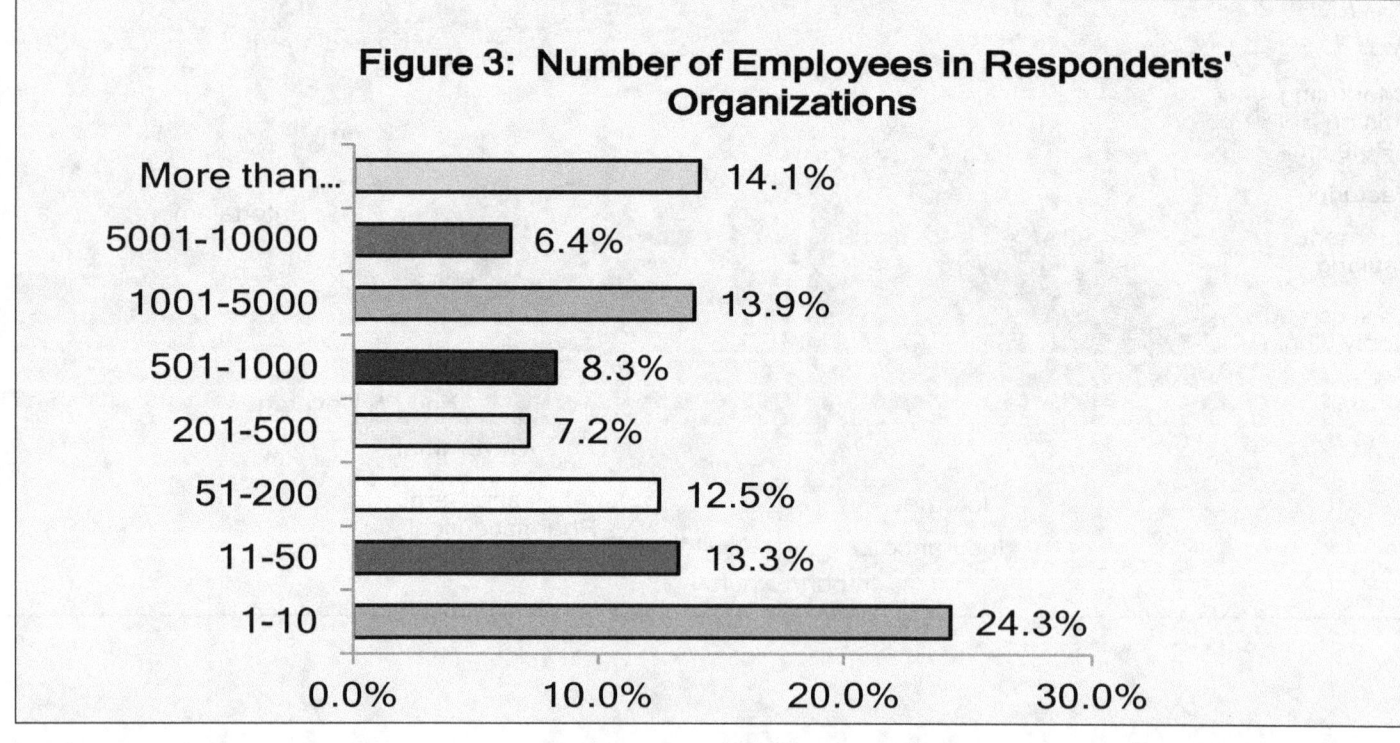

The survey also encompassed a global range of companies. While the respondents were primarily headquartered in the United States (approximately 85%) and the European Union (approximately 9%), satellite offices showed a more global distribution.

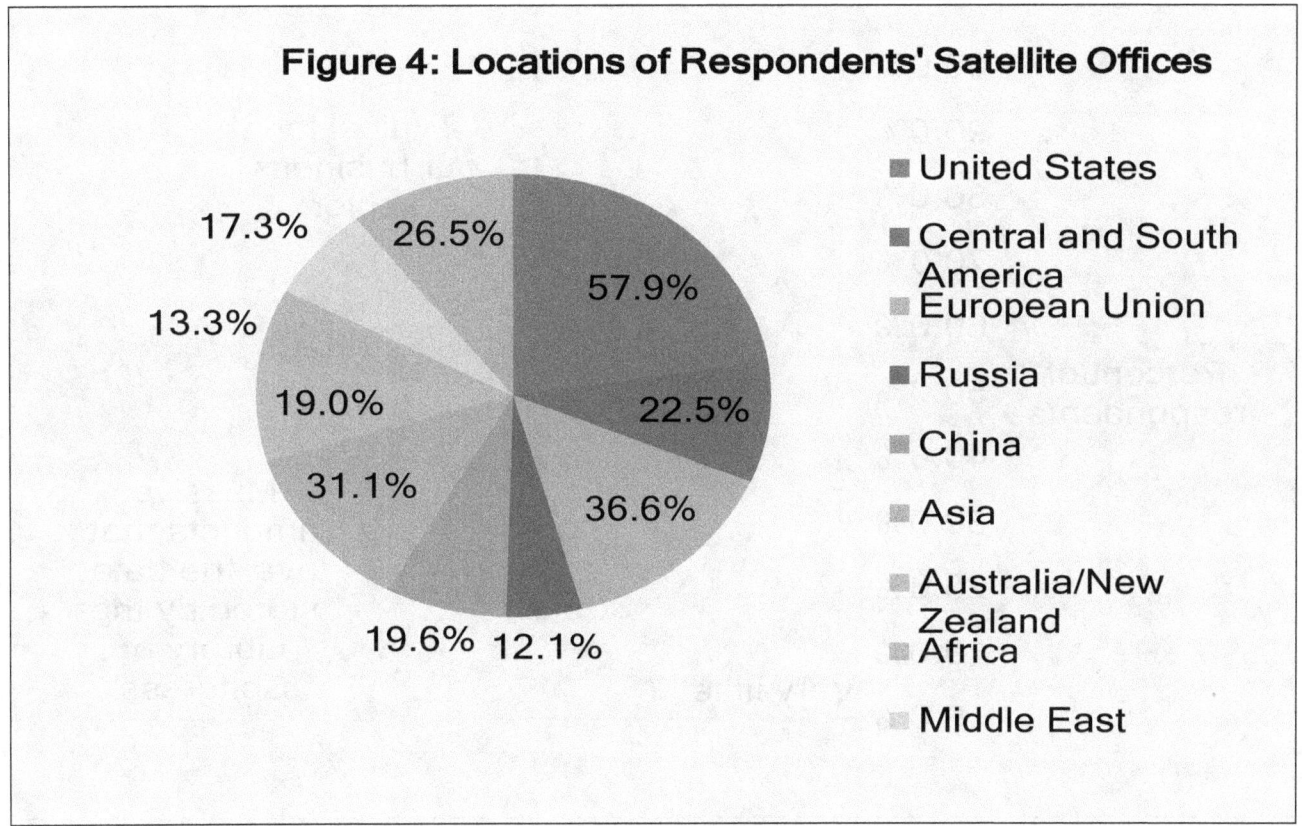

Finally, the survey encompassed a range of data usage. While the majority of respondents reported a data generated/retained typical for their business sector, nearly 11% reported "[m]assive amounts that rival the data stored by the Library of Congress."

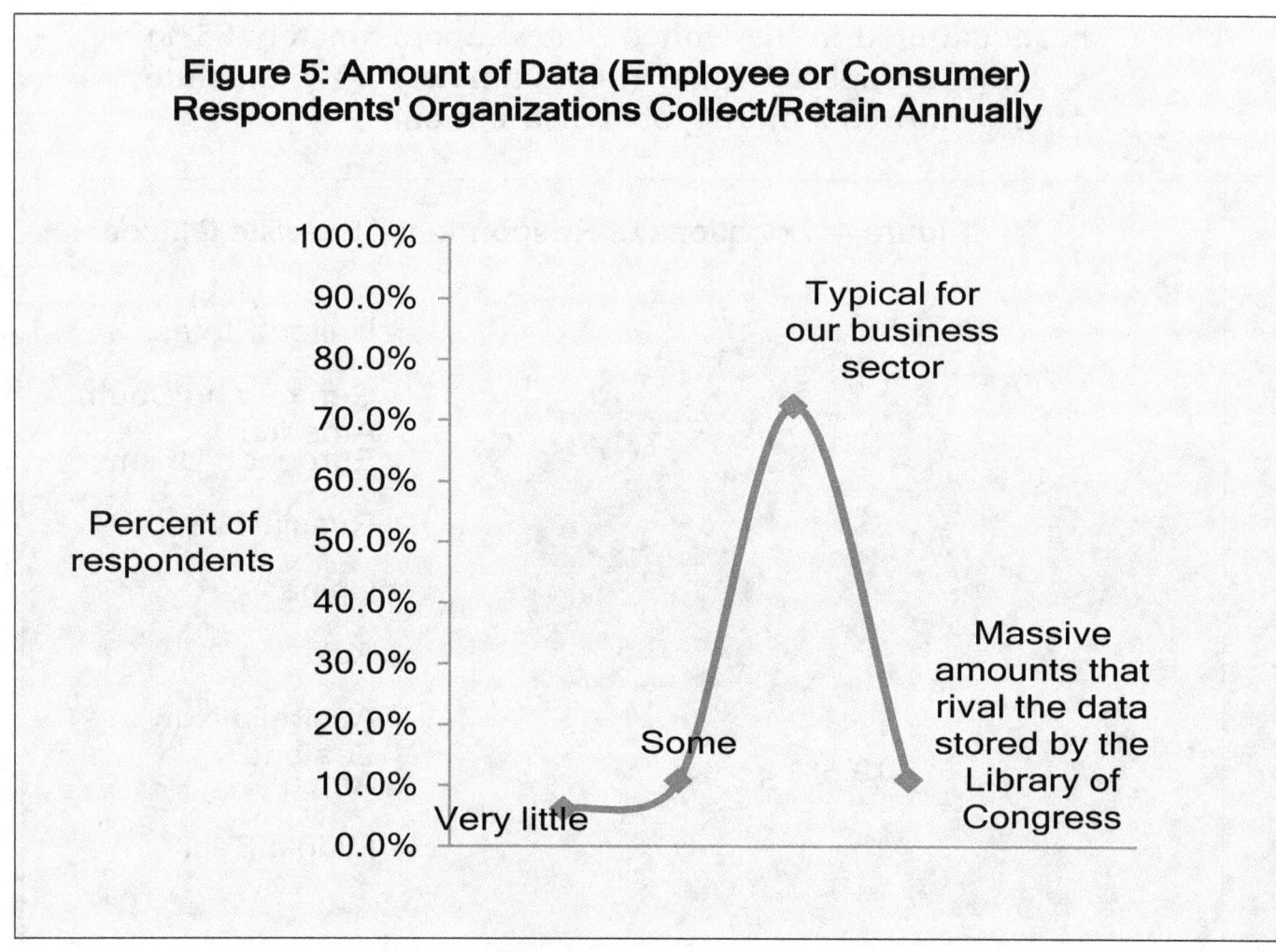

Figure 5: Amount of Data (Employee or Consumer) Respondents' Organizations Collect/Retain Annually

B. Key Findings

1. Big Data is Pervasive

Respondents who reported generating or using data in "massive amounts" rivaling the data "stored by the Library of Congress" came from several industries.

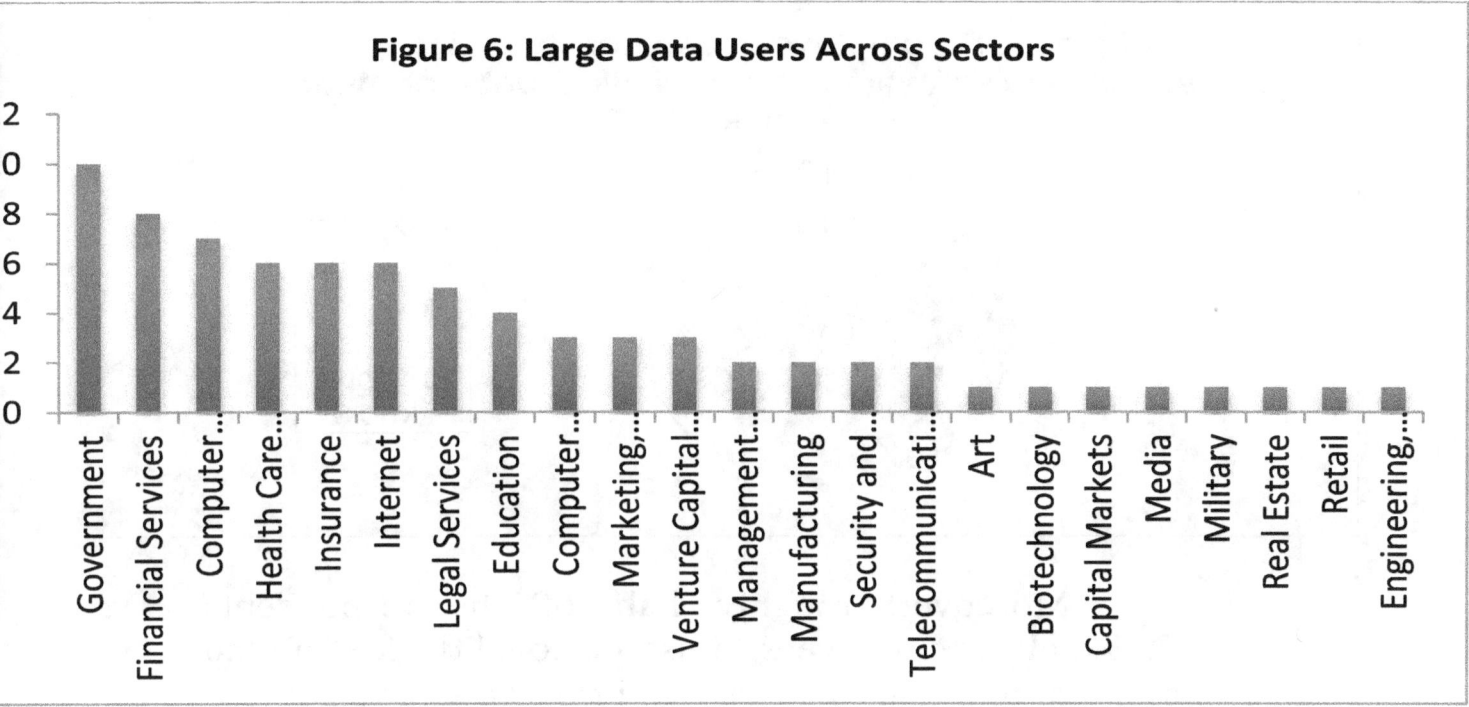

Figure 6: Large Data Users Across Sectors

The sectors represented among the heaviest data users show a concentration in government, financial services, software, health care, insurance, and internet, but surprisingly also include sectors as disparate as art, biotechnology, and manufacturing. This finding highlights the pervasiveness of large data usage across business sectors.

2. Inconsistent Knowledge and Use of IT Systems

The survey responses demonstrate that many businesses operate without meaningful security protocols, failing to monitor employee-data usage and leaving themselves vulnerable to a hacking attempt.

Nearly half of respondents acknowledged that employees use non-sanctioned software to transmit files, with roughly 15% of respondents not aware of use of such software.

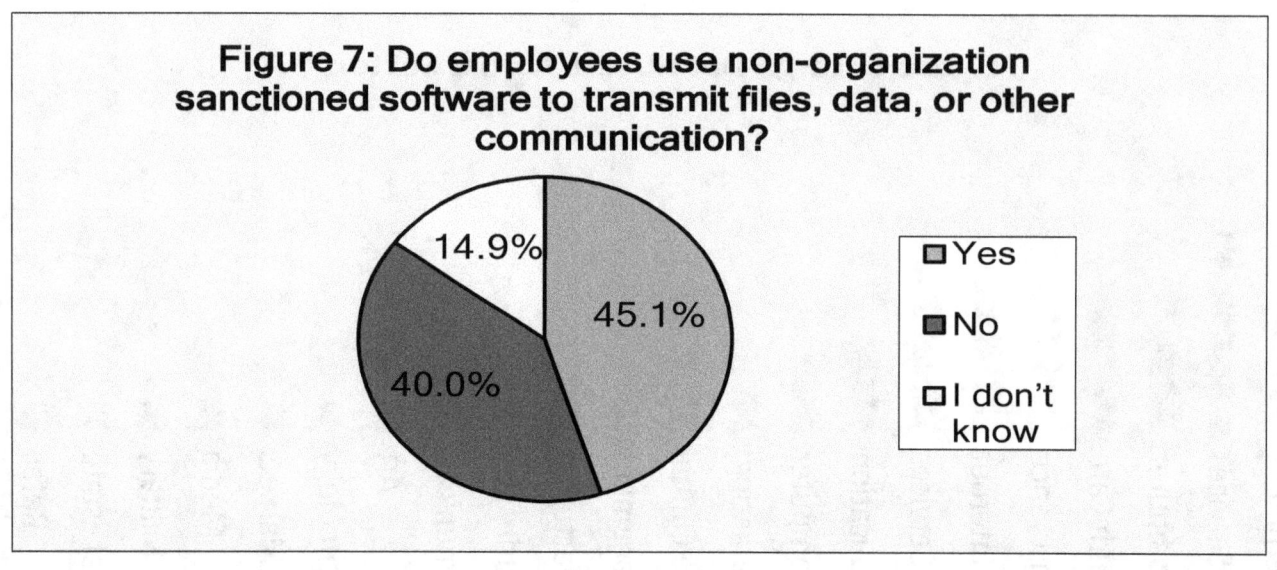

Figure 7: Do employees use non-organization sanctioned software to transmit files, data, or other communication?

- Yes: 45.1%
- No: 40.0%
- I don't know: 14.9%

Moreover, roughly half of the respondents (48.8%) allow employees to use personal devices on the corporate network, i.e. use a bring-your-own device ("BYOD") policy, while a minority (8.4%) did not know whether a BYOD policy was in place. Among respondents with a BYOD policy, only one-third stated that they monitor employee-data usage across the corporate network.

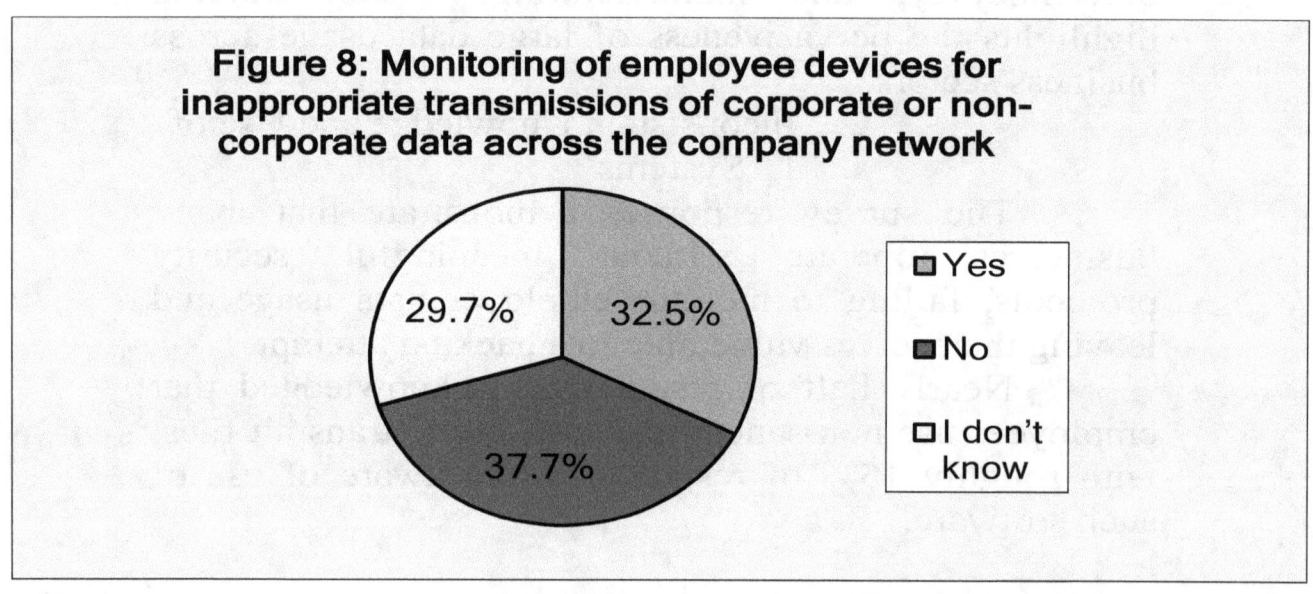

Figure 8: Monitoring of employee devices for inappropriate transmissions of corporate or non-corporate data across the company network

- Yes: 32.5%
- No: 37.7%
- I don't know: 29.7%

However, despite pervasive BYOD policies and employee use of non-sanctioned software, almost half of the respondents (48.3%) provide no training to employees to recognize hacking events.

3. Under-Reporting of Hacks

As a whole, respondents overwhelmingly did not report hacks to authorities, and in the context of pervasive under-monitoring and minimal information security and other findings discussed below, it is very likely that hacks and leaks are under-reported.

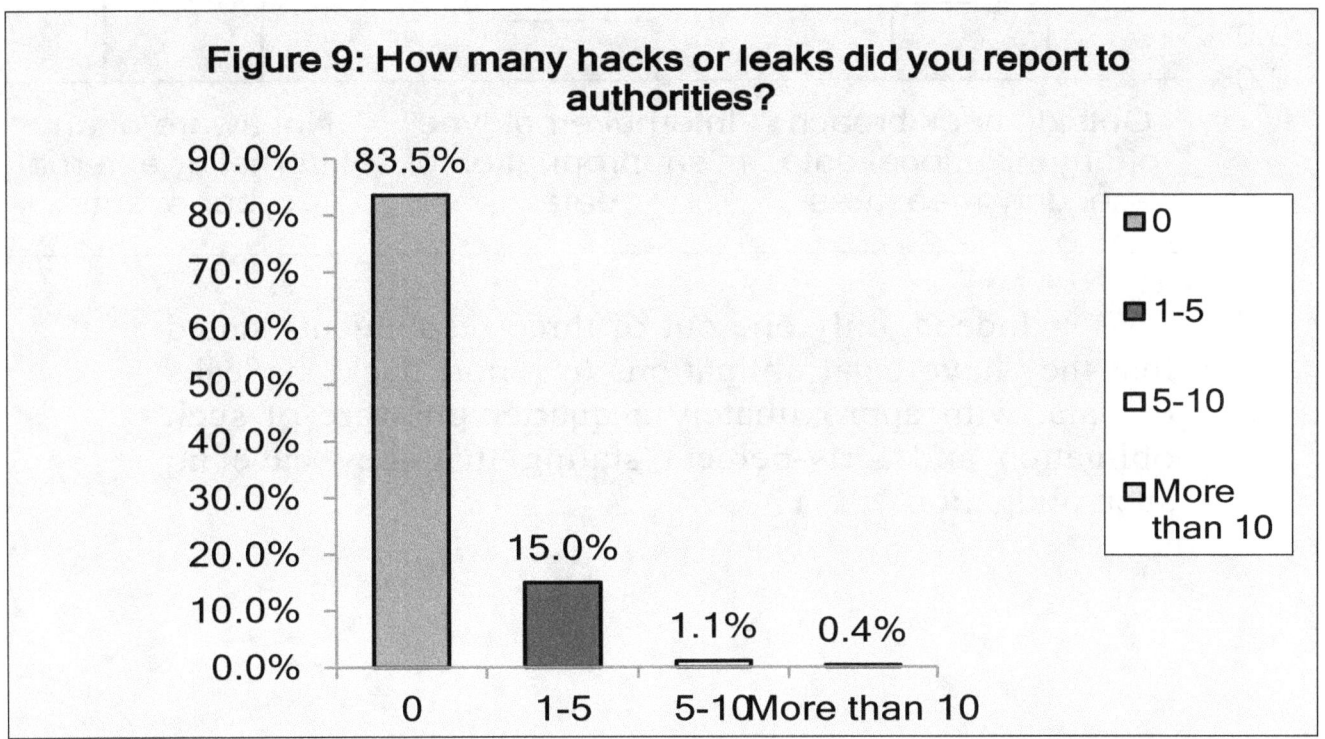

Roughly one in five respondents are aware of a hack or leak in the last three years, however the vast majority report being unaware of any internal or external hacks or leaks in that time.

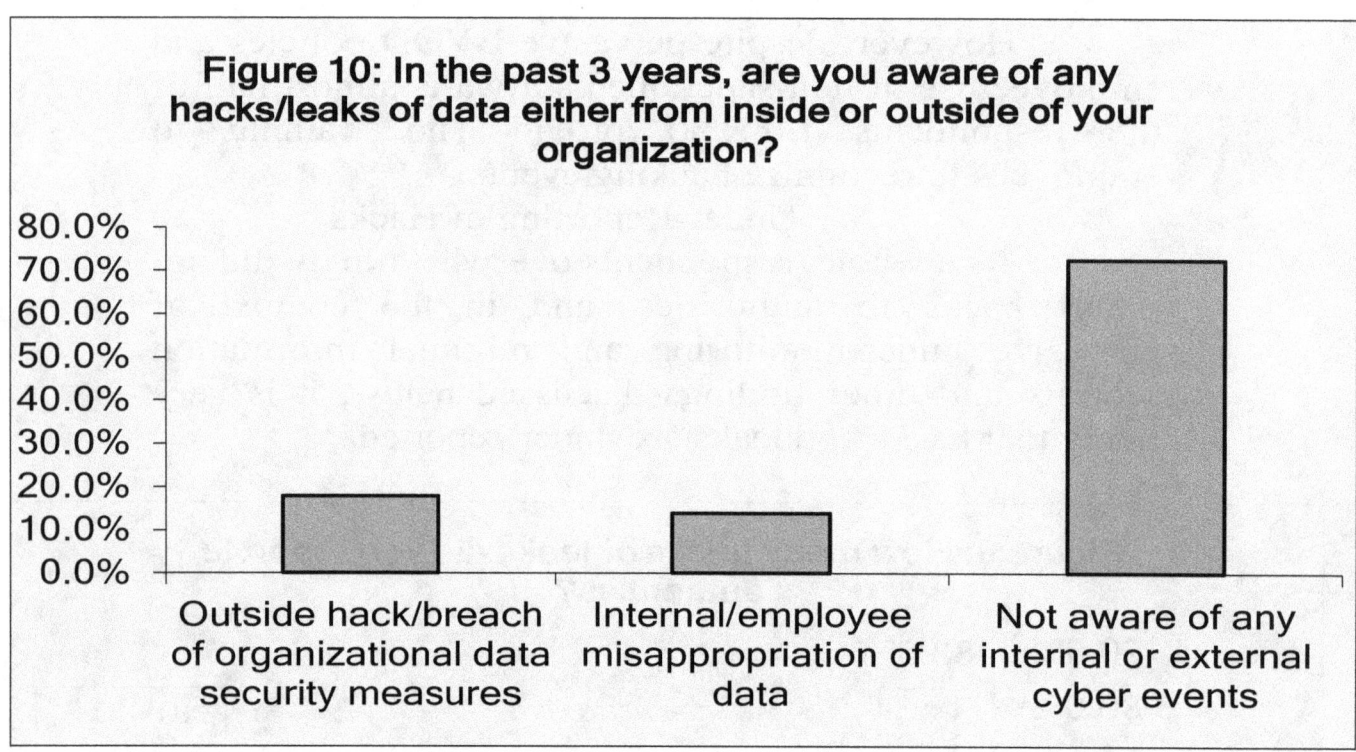

Indeed, only one out of three respondents stated that they have legal obligations to report hacks or leaks of data, with approximately a quarter unaware of such obligation and forty-percent stating that they have no such obligation.

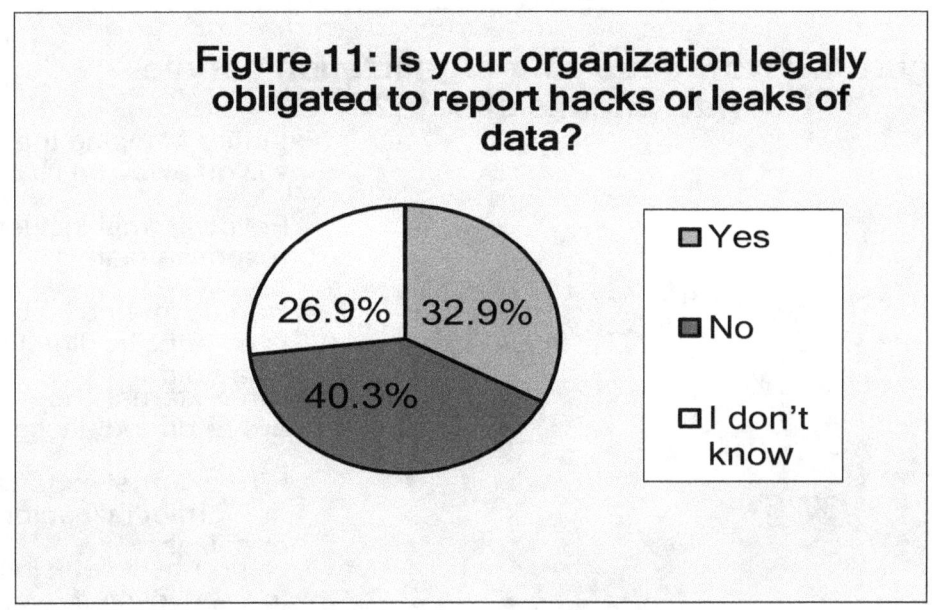

Figure 11: Is your organization legally obligated to report hacks or leaks of data?

Although half of respondents have a formal incident-response plan in place, a large percentage (42.3%) attempt to handle incident response internally with no specific direction, while more than seven percent admit to ignoring incidents entirely. In addition, very few organizations (7.3%) publicly report any hacks or leaks, although some do report to outside stakeholders or law enforcement.

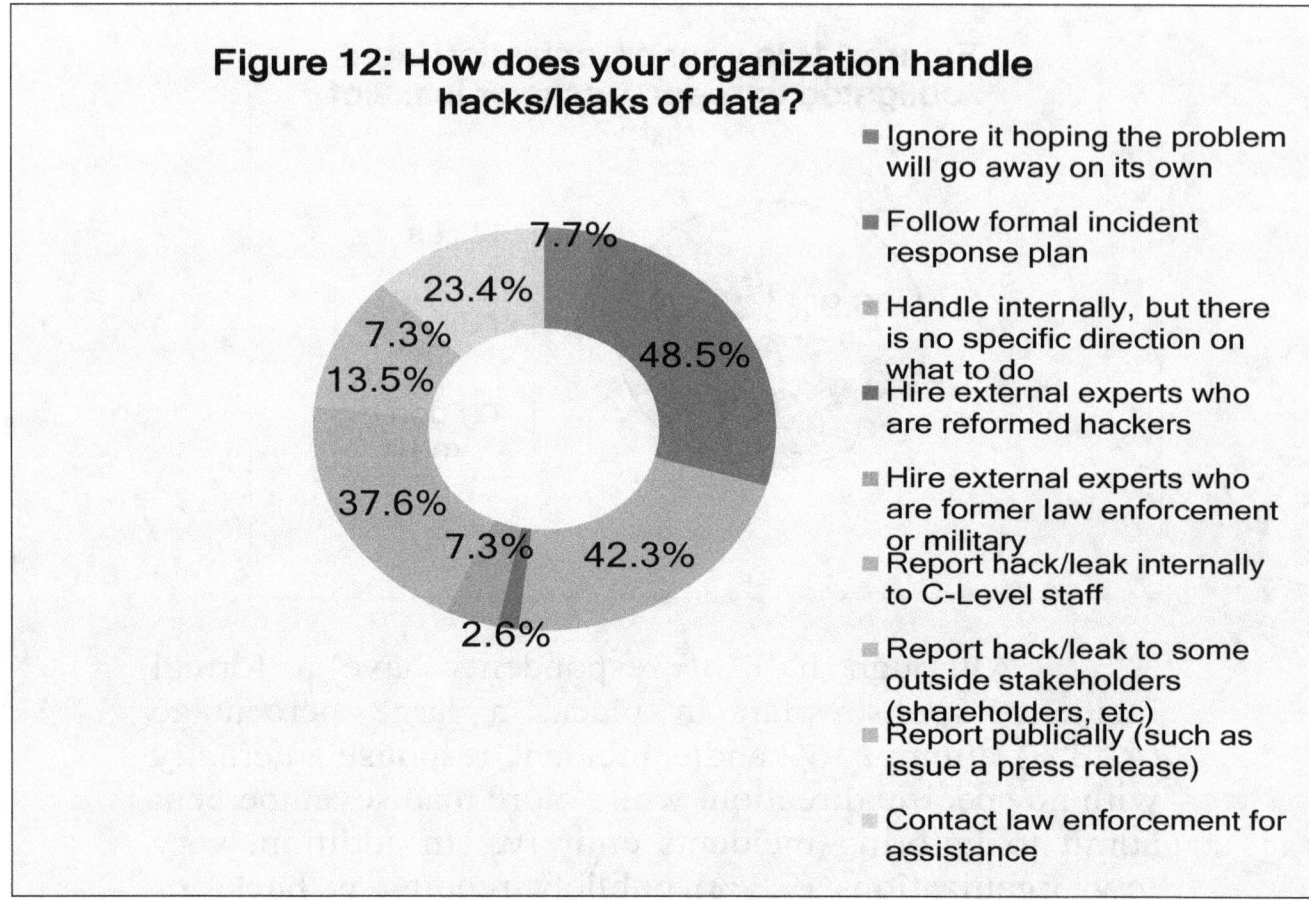

These findings strongly suggest that organizations encounter far more hacks and leaks than are reported and organizations are largely unaware of the frequency of such hacks and leaks. Nonetheless, and unconvincingly, most organizations state that they do not suspect that there have been undetected hacks or leaks.

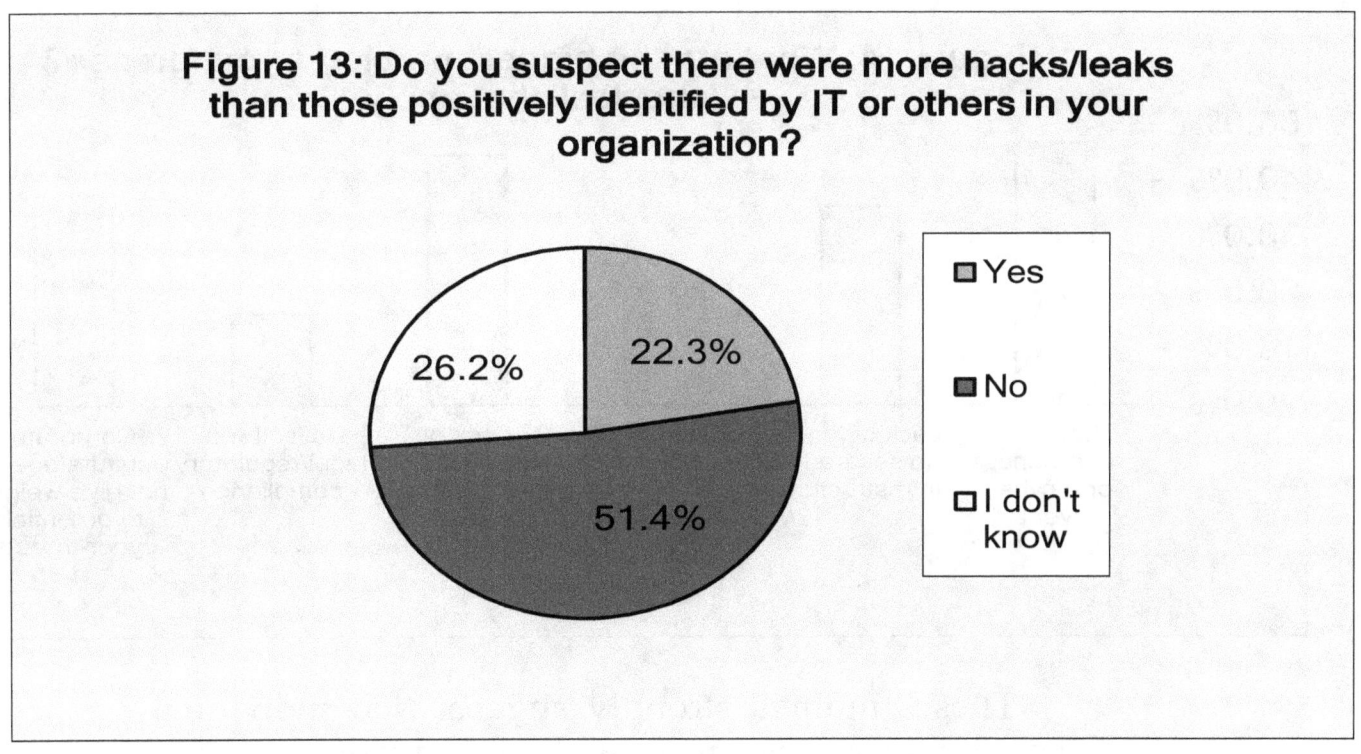

Figure 13: Do you suspect there were more hacks/leaks than those positively identified by IT or others in your organization?

Indeed, while a majority (59.2%) of respondent believe that their *industry* is ripe for hacking, about half (50.9%) of organizations do not think that they *specifically* face hacking risk, while most (60.1%) believe they are adequately managing data security. In contrast, the biggest problems respondents see are lack of preparedness for a hack or leak followed by lack of information about threats, and an indifferent corporate attitude respectively.

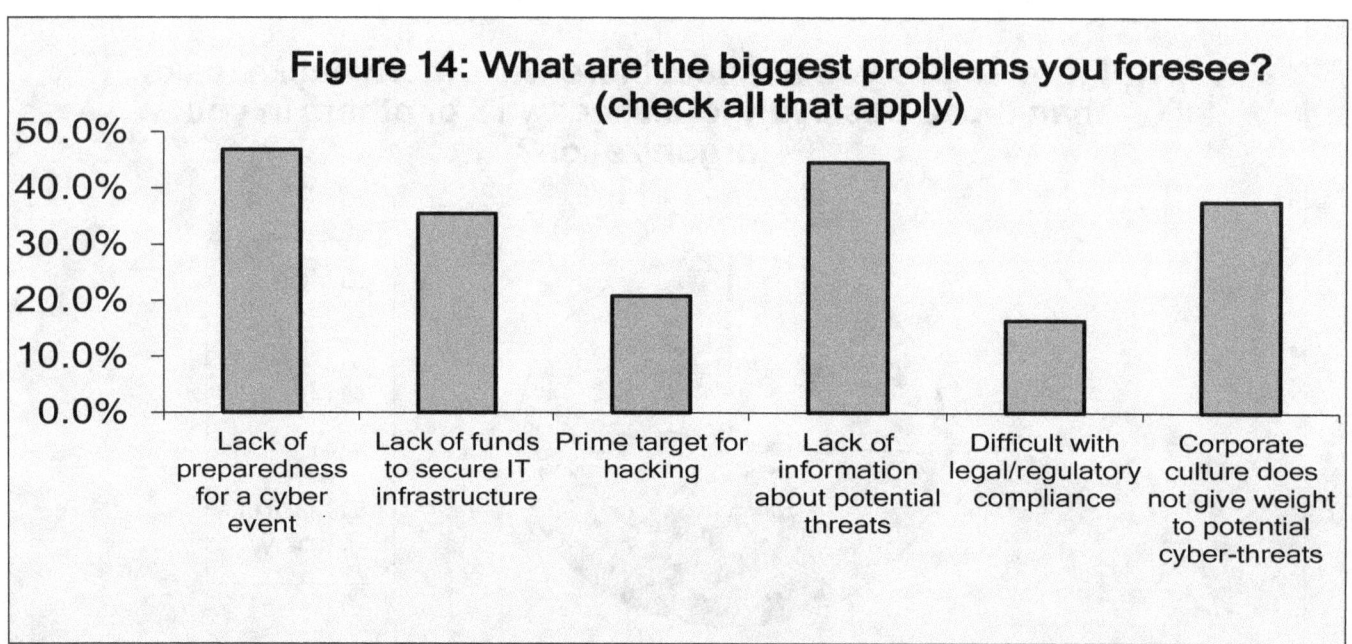

These findings strongly suggest that individual business organizations are unwilling to recognize their level of cyber risk, even as they acknowledge the risks in their industries. In other words, there appears to be a high level of "cyber risk denial" across many industries.

C. Proposed Regulatory Solution

Although respondents were apparently naive about their own organizations' risk of hacking, JLCW's survey respondents did overwhelmingly express a desire for increased and more consistent federal involvement in cyber issues. However, respondents were inconsistent in their calls for federal involvement with some asking for a federal "response kit," others proposing federally funded research, others proposing that legal remedies against hackers be implemented, and still others expressing skepticism that any federal involvement could grapple with the business risks.

The Journal here proposes a legal solution that draws from pre-existing models in anti-money laundering and insurance payments in asbestos bankruptcy litigation. These models advance objectives relevant to cyber warfare: first facilitating information sharing by creating confidential reporting mechanisms; and second ensuring that funds exist to pay claimants. In short, the Journal proposes that, when a business discovers it has been targeted by cyber hackers, it should file a claim confidentially with a (new or pre-existing) federal agency, similar to suspicious activity reporting by financial institutions. Second, if certain criteria are met, the agency would enter a channeling injunction channeling liability from the company to a trust that would be funded to ensure appropriate payments to claimants for claims arising out of the incident. This injunction could be modeled after the Bankruptcy Code's 524(g) injunction developed in the asbestos litigation context.

Following the events of September 11, 2001 and the passage of the Patriot Act, financial institutions came under close scrutiny as possible vehicles for money laundering and terrorist financing. Financial institutions were subject to expanded reporting obligations requiring them to notify the Financial Crimes Enforcement Network ("FinCEN") of transaction activity suggestive of criminal behavior, money laundering, or terrorist financing by filing a suspicious activity report or "SAR." This post-September 11th regulatory environment resulted in a massive increase in SAR reporting by financial institutions.[20]

To facilitate this reporting and prevent targets of such reporting from discovering that they had been identified, the Bank Secrecy Act ("BSA") prohibits financial institutions from disclosing the contents of a SAR or even its existence to persons involved in the

---

[20] "The SAR Activity Review," By the Numbers, Issue 8, FinCEN (June 2007).

transactions.[21] Other banking agency regulations expand this confidentiality privilege[22] and shield financial institutions from liability for reporting such activity.[23] These regulations promote information sharing between financial institutions and regulators by shielding SAR-reporting activity from discovery in civil litigation and limiting liability to financial institutions for reporting suspicious activity.

Such regulations provide a useful model for cyber-hacking reporting because the same concerns apply. In cyber warfare, regulators have an interest in sharing information with businesses, but businesses currently have many disincentives to engage in such reporting, including potential reputational damage and adverse regulatory action.[24] A regulatory regime that allowed for confidential reporting and limited liability, as the SAR reporting regime does, would address these concerns.

Similarly, a model already exists within bankruptcy law which would address other issues in cyber warfare. This model is the 524(g) channeling

---

[21] Financial institutions and their directors, officers, employees, or agents "may not notify any person involved in the transaction that the transaction has been reported." 31 U.S.C. § 5318(g)(2)(A)(i).

[22] 12 C.F.R. § 21.11(k) (stating that "any national bank or person subpoenaed or otherwise requested to disclose a SAR or the information contained in a SAR shall decline to produce the SAR or to provide any information that would disclose that a SAR has been prepared or filed.")

[23] 31 U.S.C. § 5318(g)(3); 31 C.F.R. § 103.18(e) (Department of Treasury/FinCEN); 12 C.F.R. § 21.11(l) (Office of Currency Comptroller); 12 C.F.R. § 563.180(d)(13) (Office of Thrift Supervision); 12 C.F.R. § 358.3(h) (FDIC); 12 C.F.R. § 208.62(k) (Federal Reserve Board).

[24] Some publicly traded companies engage in limited reporting of cyber incidents pursuant to their obligation to report "material information" and "material developments." However, these companies face the same disincentives to full reporting identified above.

injunction, which is used when a business files for bankruptcy after facing mass tort claims, usually for asbestos. In such a situation, where a business may be unable to pay liabilities to all present and future claimants, a 524(g) injunction channels liability from the bankruptcy debtor to a trust funded by the debtor and its insurers. The trust is administered by a trustee who works to ensure that funds are used appropriately to pay claimants. Congress created 524(g) as part of the Bankruptcy Reform Act of 1994 to codify the trust and injunction used in the Chapter 11 bankruptcies of *In re Johns-Manville Corp.* The *Manville* court relied on its general equitable powers under Bankruptcy Code section 105(a) in issuing the channeling injunction. However investors were unsure of the legality of this mechanism and were unwilling to purchase stock in the reorganized debtor for fear of possible liabilities to undisclosed future claimants. Confidence further deteriorated after the Manville trust declared insolvency. Accordingly, Congress created 524(g) to provide certainty to businesses faced with mass asbestos liability and ensure their ability to reorganize under Chapter 11.

This model provides many attractive features to a business that has been the victim of a cyber incident and now faces present and potentially future customer claims. The prospect of facing potentially thousands of claims may inhibit business' incentives to report cyber incidents and also poses logistical problems for the business. The creation of a trust under the aegis of a federal agency would allow businesses to move forward after a cyber incident while ensuring claimants are appropriately redressed. Such a mechanism may also promote more open reporting of cyber incidents by businesses as well as promote the growth of the cyber insurance market.

D. Conclusion

The findings above reveal that many businesses remain almost willfully ignorant of cyber-security risks. Many organizations prefer to hope that they do not face risks, even as they acknowledge lack of monitoring and training, lack of resources, indifferent corporate attitudes and industry-wide risks.

Moreover, it is clear that most industries lack any meaningful incentives to report hacks or leaks, which has encouraged a culture of silence precisely where information sharing would be most valuable. In this regard, many respondents cited a lack of federal oversight or regulatory mechanisms as a problem in managing cyber risk.

The Journal has proposed what it believes to be a viable framework for such a federal program. In any event, in the absence of such federal oversight, JLCW's Cyber Security Survey results strongly suggest that organizations need to raise internal awareness of data security issues and implement protocols to discover, report, and remedy hacks and leaks.

Cyberwarfare: Attribution, Preemption, and National Self Defense

By John Dever[*] and James Dever[**]

I. INTRODUCTION

In recent years, both the capability to protect against a large-scale cyberattack, and the capability to launch a successful cyberattack against another country have become an integral and ever-growing part of the

---

[*] John P. Dever Jr. holds a L.L.M. in National Security Law from Georgetown University. He is the Global Crisis Management Leader at GE. He was also an Assistant U.S. Attorney, and prior to that, he was Assistant General Counsel in the Federal Bureau of Investigation's National Security Law Branch, Counterterrorism Division. He began his career as a U.S. Army Judge Advocate. He has served multiple combat deployments and is the recipient of the Bronze Star and the Purple Heart Medals.

[**] James A. Dever, Esq. holds an advanced degree in History and has worked with the Department of Homeland Security. He teaches at Quinnipiac University and is the General Counsel for a government contracting firm. He is a Judge Advocate in the U.S. Army Reserves.

national security strategy of the United States.[1] While conventional kinetic military attacks are likely to remain a mainstay of conflict for the foreseeable future, cyberattacks are rapidly becoming an attractive option as technology becomes both more sophisticated and widely accessible. This means of attack also permits a less powerful enemy, in the traditional sense of force on force engagements, to damage a stronger foe. In a fashion, it is the ultimate development in asymmetric warfare. The difficulty associated with attribution in a cyberattack makes this option ever more appealing as it is less likely to be met with a quick and deadly kinetic response. In essence, cyberspace may become a relatively safe haven from which to launch attacks.[2] The *2010 National Security Strategy* emphasized that "cybersecurity threats represent one of the most serious national security, public safety, and economic challenges we face as a nation."[3] As the technology to engage in cyberattack proliferates, as appears inevitable, more actors, nations states, their proxies, non-state actors, criminal entities, and lone wolves will likely avail

---

[1] WHITEHOUSE, NATIONAL SECURITY STRATEGY 27 (2010), *available at:* http://www.whitehouse.gov/sites/default/files/rss_viewer/national_security_strategy.pdf [hereinafter, 2010 NATIONAL SECURITY STRATEGY]; U.S. DEP'T OF DEFENSE, DEPARTMENT OF DEFENSE STRATEGY FOR OPERATING IN CYBERSPACE 4, *available at:* http://www.defense.gov/home/features/2011/0411_cyberstrategy/docs/DoD_Strategy_for_Operating_in_Cyberspace_July_2011.pdf; WHITEHOUSE, WHITEHOUSE INTERNATIONAL STRATEGY FOR CYBERSPACE 12 (2011), *available at:* *http://www.whitehouse.gov/sites/default/files/rss_viewer/internationalstrategy_cyberspace.pdf* [hereinafter 2011 INTERNATIONAL STRATEGY FOR CYBERSPACE].

[2] LIEUTENANT COLONEL SCOTT W. BEIDLEMAN, DEFINING AND DETERRING CYBER WAR 21, *available at:* http://www.dtic.mil/cgi-bin/GetTRDoc?AD=ADA500795.

[3] 2010 NATIONAL SECURITY STRATEGY, *supra* note 2 at 27.

themselves of this technology, thereby increasing the threat picture to the United States.[4] These cyberattacks may eventually have a disproportionate impact, allowing those who seek to harm the United States destructive ability without the advanced weapons systems they would have once needed.[5]

The importance of cybersecurity to the United States was highlighted in the *2010 National Security Strategy*, where it was emphasized that protecting U.S. national security requires that the "U.S. military continues to have the necessary capabilities across all domains—land, air, sea, space, and cyber."[6] The *2010 National Security Strategy* highlighted the importance of cybersecurity to U.S. national security as a whole, and laid the foundations for the development of the *Department of Defense Strategy for Operating in Cyberspace*, and the *May 2011 Whitehouse International Strategy for Cyberspace*, which further emphasize the importance of cybersecurity.[7] In particular, the *May 2011 Whitehouse International Strategy for Cyberspace* advocates that "states have an inherent right to self-defense that may be triggered by certain aggressive acts in cyberspace,"[8] and that "[w]hen warranted, the United States will respond to hostile acts in cyberspace as [it]

---

[4] JAMES ANDREW LEWIS, CYBER ATTACKS, REAL OR IMAGINED, AND CYBER WAR, http://csis.org/publication/cyber-attacks-real-or-imagined-and-cyber-war,

[5] U.S. DEP'T OF DEFENSE, DEPARTMENT OF DEFENSE STRATEGY FOR OPERATING IN CYBERSPACE 3 (2011), *available at:* http://www.defense.gov/home/features/2011/0411_cyberstrategy/docs/DoD_Strategy_for_Operating_in_Cyberspace_July_2011.pdf. [hereinafter 2011 DEPARTMENT OF DEFENSE CYBERSPACE STRATEGY].

[6] 2010 NATIONAL SECURITY STRATEGY, *supra* note 2 at 22

[7] 2011 DEPARTMENT OF DEFENSE CYBERSPACE STRATEGY, *supra* note 6 at 4; 2011 INTERNATIONAL STRATEGY FOR CYBERSPACE, *supra* note 2 at 12.

[8] 2011 INTERNATIONAL STRATEGY FOR CYBERSPACE, *supra* note 2 at 10.

would to any other threat to our country," including the use of military force.[9]

Despite the emphasis on the importance of cybersecurity in policy documents, there has been little discussion about when a cyberattack on the U.S. or conducted by the U.S. on another country becomes more than just interference in another country's affairs, and reaches the level of an armed attack that can be responded to in self-defense.[10] Indeed, the law of cyberattacks still retains the frameworks and tests applicable to traditional warfare. Such frameworks, however, using concepts such as "armed force" or "aggression" are inadequate analogies to address the nuances of cyber attacks. Therefore, this paper proposes a new consequentialist standard based on an "Effects Test" to define when cyberattacks constitute an armed attack that can be responded to in self-defense. This paper will also address the use of anticipatory self-defense in the cyber context by proposing a modification of the traditional *Caroline* doctrine using a court system as a check on abuse of the anticipatory self-defense doctrine.

II. CYBERATTACKS

In order to determine what legal regime should be used to combat cyberattacks, it is important to understand the many forms they take. One of the most difficult aspects of defining cyberattacks is the large amount of diversity among those acts that can be considered cyberattacks. A cyberattack broadly encompasses "the use of deliberate actions—perhaps over an extended period of time—to alter, disrupt, deceive, degrade, or destroy adversary computer systems or networks or the information and/or programs resident

---

[9] *Id.* at 14.
[10] *Id.* at 9 (discussing that new international norms are needed in the cybersecurity context but not stating what that new norms might be).

in or transiting these systems or networks."[11] In addition, the nature and seriousness of a cyberattack can vary based on the actors involved, the way in which the attack is conducted, what the result of the attack is.[12] Cyberattacks can include something as small as an individual hacking into the computer of another individual to obtain the person's banking information, or something as large scale as one country taking control of another country's military computers and firing that country's weapons, and all the possible activity that falls in between.[13]

III. CURRENT LEGAL FRAMEWORK

Determining when a cyberattack constitutes an armed attack is important in three contexts within the U.N. Charter framework, the first of which is a legal question, whereas the other two are policy questions that would need to be determined by the U.N. Security Council. First, it is important in determining whether an act will constitute an armed attack that a country can respond to in self-defense, second it is important in determining whether a cyberattack constitutes a threat to the peace, breach of the peace, or an act of aggression under Article 39, and third it is important in determining whether a cyberattack, when used by the Security Council to respond to a threat to the peace, breach of the peace, or an act of aggression, should be classified only as the use of force allowed under Article 42, or an action that does not constitute the use of force under Article 41. While the first context is perhaps the most important because it establishes a legal framework, but the second

---

[11] KENNETH W. DAM, ET AL., TECHNOLOGY, POLICY, LAW, AND ETHICS REGARDING U.S. ACQUISITION AND USE OF CYBERATTACK CAPABILITIES 80 (2009).

[12] Matthew C. Waxman, *Cyber-Attacks and the Use of Force: Back to the Future of Article 2(4)*, 36 YALE J. INT'L L. 421, 422 (2011).

[13] *Id.* at 422-23.

two contexts demonstrate the power that the U.N. Security Council has to make decisions concerning various types of actions, whether an individual state can respond to that action, or whether the United Nations as a whole can respond. While two of the contexts involve a policy decision being made, instead of a legal decision, the guidance that can be provided through the definition of an armed attack can be useful in helping the Security Council make those policy decisions, and therefore limit the confusion among states about what is permissible with regards to cyberattacks.

A. ARTICLE 2(4) AND ARTICLE 51

The first context in which it is necessary to determine whether a cyberattack constitutes the use of force is with regards to the prohibition of the use of force. Under Article 2(4) of the U.N. Charter, "[a]ll members shall refrain in their international relations from the threat or use of force against the territorial integrity or political independence of any state, or in any other manner inconsistent with the Purposes of the United Nations."[14] This provides for a general prohibition on a country using physical force on another country, and therefore it is necessary to determine whether a cyberattack constitutes the use of force to determine whether any type of cyberattack is permissible under the U.N. Charter. Due to large variety in size and scope of cyberattacks, it is unlikely that every cyberattack would be considered to be the use of force, but the difficulty is in determining where to draw the line. For instance, stealing someone's personal information would be considered a cyberattack, but would not be considered to be the use of force. Within the U.N. Charter there is only one exception to the prohibition on the use of force established by Article

---

[14] U.N. Charter art. 2, para. 4.

2(4), and that is the right of self-defense under Article 51.[15] Article 51 states that:

> Nothing in the present Charter shall impair the inherent right of individual or collective self-defence if an armed attack occurs against a Member of the United Nations, until the Security Council has taken measures necessary to maintain international peace and security. Measures taken by Members in the exercise of this right of self-defence shall be immediately reported to the Security Council and shall not in any way affect the authority and responsibility of the Security Council under the present Charter to take at any time such action as it deems necessary in order to maintain or restore international peace and security.[16]

The right to self-defense is not unlimited under Article 51 because to act in self-defense, one must have been subjected to an armed attack.[17] The question then becomes what is an armed attack. What constitutes an armed attack is not specifically defined within the U.N. Charter, but the International Court of Justice (ICJ) has explored this issue in a few of its decisions.[18] In the Nicaragua case, the ICJ determined that it is necessary to distinguish between the gravest forms of the use of

---

[15] U.N. Charter art. 2, para. 4, art. 51.
[16] U.N. Charter art. 51.
[17] *Id.*
[18] *Military and Paramilitary Activities in and Against Nicaragua (Nicaragua v. U.S.)*, 1986 I.C.J. 14, ¶¶ 191, 210-211 (June 27); Oil Platforms (Islamic Republic of Iran vs. U.S.), 2003 I.C.J. 161, ¶¶ 51, 64 (November 6).

force, those constituting an armed attack, and other less grave forms.[19] While the use of force is allowed when responding in self-defense to an armed attack, the use of force is not allowed when merely responding to another state's intervention that does not reach the level of an armed attack.[20] The same principles were reiterated in the Oil Platform case, in which the court found that the actions of the Iranians did not rise to the level of an armed attack, and therefore the U.S. had no right to respond with force in self-defense.[21] While ICJ guidance on these issues is somewhat ambiguous, it is clear that it has held that the right to respond in self-defense is allowed in response to all forms of the use of force, but only the use of force that is considered to be an armed attack.[22] Within the cybersecurity context, this is a difficult distinction to draw.

B. ARTICLE 39

The second context in which it is necessary to determine whether a cyberattack constitutes an armed attack, is when determining whether a given action constitutes a threat to the peace, breach of the peace, or an act of aggression under Article 39.[23] Under Article 39 of the U.N. Charter,

> [t]he Security Council shall determine the existence of any threat to the peace, breach of the peace, or act of aggression and shall make recommendations, or decide what measures shall be taken in accordance with Articles 41 and 42, to

---

[19] *Nicaragua*, 1986 I.C.J. 14, at ¶ 191.
[20] *Id.* at ¶ 210-211.
[21] *Oil Platforms*, 2003 I.C.J. 161 at ¶¶ 51, 64.
[22] *Nicaragua*, 1986 I.C.J. 14, at ¶¶ 210-211; *Oil Platforms*, 2003 I.C.J. 161, at ¶¶ 51, 64.
[23] U.N. Charter art. 39.

maintain or restore international peace and security."[24]

While the U.N. Charter allows for the U.N. Security Council to declare whether a specific act constitutes a threat to the peace, breach of the peace, or an act of aggression, there are no definitions of these specific terms in the Charter itself, and it is left up to the U.N. Security Council to determine both what these terms mean, and whether a particular action fits into one of these categories.[25] Therefore, what actions constitute a threat to the peace, a breach of the peace, or an act of aggression constitutes a policy decision by the Security Council.[26] The failure to have clear definitions makes it difficult for states to determine whether their actions are allowed by the Security Council prior to actually committing the actions. This is particularly true in the context of an emerging field, such as cyberspace. Having a definition that defines what would be an act of aggression within the cyberspace context would help states to ensure that they do not engage in these types of activities, and prevent conflict. In U.N. Resolution 3341, the General Assembly defined aggression as "the first use of armed force by a State in contravention with the Charter...although the Security Council may...conclude that a determination that a act of aggression has been committed would not be justified in the light of other relevant circumstances."[27] Resolution 3341 then goes on to list a number of possible actions that might constitute an act of aggression, and all of these examples include the use of armed force.[28] The

---

[24] *Id.*
[25] *Id.*
[26] *Id.*
[27] G.A. Res. 3314 (XXIX), U.N. GAOR, 29th Session (December 14, 1974).
[28] *Id.*

issue of what constitutes an act of aggression was revisited at the Kampala Review Conference of the Rome Statute in 2010, and Article 8 of the Rome Statute was amended to include a definition of what constitutes an act of aggression under the Rome Statute, and again requires the use of armed force.[29] Under both the U.N. General Assembly and the Rome Statute's definition of an act of aggression, an act of aggression requires the use of some sort of armed force, which results in complications in the cyberspace context because straightforward analogies cannot be made to any of the examples of the use of force provided.[30]

Although the determination about whether a cyberattack constitutes an act of aggression under Article 39 is a policy decision by the Security Council it would provide greater clarity in the international context if there were a more clearly defined standard, which separates in a distinct manner armed attack, aggression, and use of force.[31]

C. ARTICLE 41 AND 42

The third context in which it is necessary to determine whether a cyberattack constitutes an armed attack, is when the U.N. Security Council is deciding how to respond to a threat to the peace, breach of the peace, or an act of aggression, and if they decide to respond with a cyberattack, whether this action would be a response under Article 41 or Article 42 of the U.N. Charter.[32] Article 41 provides the Security Council with the ability to conduct measures not involving the use of

---

[29] Rome Statute of the International Criminal Court art. 8, July 17, 1998, 2187 U.N.T.S. 90.
[30] G.A. Res. 3314 (XXIX), U.N. GAOR, 29th Session (December 14, 1974); Rome Statute of the International Criminal Court art. 8, July 17, 1998, 2187 U.N.T.S. 90.
[31] U.N. Charter art. 39.
[32] U.N. Charter art. 41-42.

armed force, whereas Article 42 provides the Security Council with the ability to conduct measures using armed force when the measures under Article 41 would be inadequate or have proved to be inadequate.[33] Because of the variety in size and scope of the possible cyberattacks that could be conducted to respond to a threat to the peace, breach of the peace or an act of aggression, it would be impossible to put cyberattacks solely within Article 41 and 42, but also very difficult to determine where to draw the line as to which types of cyberattacks would be considered measures under Article 41 and which would be considered measures under Article 42.[34]

These three contexts in which the concept of an armed attack arises within the U.N. framework highlights the need for an alternative framework to handle cyberattacks because cyberattacks struggle to fit within the these frameworks in a meaningful way that can account for the diversity in the size and scopes of possible cyber attacks. In addition, it seems that under the current framework cyberattacks would very rarely constitute an armed attack or even an act of aggression because they do not appear to cross the ICJ's admittedly less than clear threshold of use of force or aggression, and because they do not usually involve armed forces in the conventional senses, and because it is difficult to make an analogy between cyberattacks that do not actually involve the use of weapons, and conventional acts that involve armed forces. Due to the fact that the current standards are difficult to apply in the cyberspace context in a meaningful way it is necessary to explore different possible frameworks to define when a cyberattack constitutes an armed attack that a country may respond to with self-defense.

---

[33] *Id.*
[34] *Id.*

IV. Proposal for a New Legal Framework, The Effects Test

While there are those who believe that the current framework can be interpreted in ways that include cyberattacks, it seems clear that the current framework really does not take into account the broad spectrum of actions that can constitute a cyberattack, and limits those actions that might constitute an armed attack to a very small number. In response to the issues highlighted by the current framework, the Effects Test has been developed as the proposed alternative approach to looking at whether a cyberattack is an armed attack.[35] This test is intended to be broad enough to be able to more effectively analyze a wider variety of cyberattacks, while still limiting the number of cyberattacks that would be considered armed attacks. Under the Effects Test, a cyberattack is an armed attack if its consequences are those which would also be seen in a conventional attack.[36] This is evaluated based on several factors, including (1) the severity of the harm caused, (2) the immediacy of the effects, (3) the directness of the effects, (4) the invasiveness of the act that caused the attack, (5) the measurability of the consequences of the attack, and (6) the presumptive legitimacy of the actions taken that caused the harm.[37] By looking at the effects of the cyberattack in the context of these six factors, one can then determine which actions constitute an armed attack based on which action has effects that are similar

---

[35] COMMITTEE ON OFFENSIVE INFORMATION WARFARE, NAT'L RESEARCH COUNCIL, TECHNOLOGY, POLICY, LAW AND ETHICS REGARDING U.S. ACQUISITION AND USE OF CYBERATTACK CAPABILITIES 33-34 (2009); Waxman, *supra*, n. 13 at 431–32.

[36] Michael Schmitt, *Computer Network Attack and the Use of Force in International Law: Thoughts on a Normative Framework*, 37 COLUM. J. TRANSNAT'L L. 885, 914 (1999).

[37] *Id.* at 914-15.

to those normally seen in an armed attack, yet with no armed forces present.[38]

V. The *Caroline* Doctrine

When addressing the issue of when the United States may respond to a cyberattack it is useful to consider historical antecedents of self-defense and consider how they would apply to the cyberattack arena. Specifically, a study of the *Caroline* case shows that a modification to the "necessity" prong of the *Caroline* test may be necessary in the cyberattack arena. Unlike the Bush Doctrine with its emphasis on preemption, a modernized *Caroline* test creates an anticipatory self-defense model that would rely heavily upon the advancement of technological capability to assist with the ever-vexing issue of attribution in the cyberattack arena. Much more attention would have to be paid to the concept of "probing" attacks, and whether such activity amounts to small scale attacks that may be compiled together and responded to with greater force.

The term "anticipatory self-defense" in the context of international law and *jus ad bellum* is commonly defined as a nation's ability to foresee the consequences of a given threat and to take proactive measures aimed at preventing those consequences.[39] Accordingly, anticipatory self-defense is distinguished from armed reprisal in that the former is protective while the latter is retributive.[40] Moreover, some legal scholars employ a further temporal analysis to differentiate between anticipatory self-defense and preemptive action. In this schema, preemptive action is where State A uses force to quell a possibility of future attack by State B even in those instances where there is no reason for State

---

[38] *Id.*
[39] Lucy Martinez, *September 11th, Iraq and the Doctrine of Anticipatory Self-Defense,* 72 UMKC L. REV. 123, 125 (2003).
[40] *Id.*

A to believe an attack by State B is planned and when no prior attack has occurred.[41] Meanwhile, anticipatory self-defense is understood as a narrower doctrine because State A must expect an imminent attack from State B.[42]

The *Caroline* incident was a dispute between the United States and the British Empire that occurred during the Canadian Rebellion of 1837.[43] The Canadian Rebellion was comprised of two regional conflicts that pitted disaffected French-Canadian smallholders against their landlords in Quebec as well as recent American immigrants to Canada against the British landed gentry in the western province of Ontario.[44] Many Americans who lived near the Canadian border sympathized with the plight of the rebels and located their struggle in terms of a second independence movement on the North American continent.[45] Yet despite the wellspring of popular support for the rebels in New York, the rebellion was defeated militarily when a poorly armed force of

---

[41] *Id.* at 125, 26.
[42] *Id.*
[43] Timothy Kearley, *Raising the Caroline,* 17 WIS. INT'L L. J. 323, 328 (1999).
[44] MICHAEL W. DOYLE, STRIKING FIRST: PREEMPTION AND PREVENTION IN INTERNATIONAL CONFLICT 11 (2008). This compilation of six essays contains an extended introduction by Dr. Stephen Macedo, Director of the Princeton University Center for Human Values, two essays by Doyle, three chapters by prominent legal authorities such as Dean Harold Hongju Koh who comment on Dr. Doyle's articulation of anticipatory self-defense, and a final rejoinder from Dr. Doyle's responses to his colleagues. The book explores these issues in a dynamic and dialectic way for a more pragmatic (less ideological) and nuanced development of the arguments.
[45] Kearley, *supra* note 44, at 328.

several hundred men were vanquished by a larger group of British militia and thereby failed to capture Toronto.[46]

Subsequent to the British victory in Ontario, rebel leader William Mackenzie fled across the border to New York where he canvassed support for a continuation of the rebellion to include procuring arms and recruiting young American and Canadian men for a "Patriot Army."[47] As one contemporary American intoned, volunteers flocked to Mackenzie's banner because "[o]nce the colonies of Great Britain, these states rebelled against her power and our fathers achieved our independence. We have considered it our boon and our birth-right to sympathize with, and fight for the oppressed. . . . The elements of revolution were ripening in the Canadas."[48] Accordingly, because the *Caroline* incident occurred during the Canadian Rebellion, it is perhaps more historically accurate to locate the event in terms of ordinary rather than anticipatory self-defense. Nonetheless, for better or worse, the process of politicization oftentimes drives collective interpretation of an event and for that reason because contemporaries understood the *Caroline* incident in terms of anticipatory self-defense, it stands for that historical proposition.

On December 13, 1837, Mackenzie and his followers established their headquarters on Navy Island, a sparsely populated settlement situated in Canadian territorial waters in the Niagara River.[49] Over the ensuing fortnight, the rebels' ranks swelled to almost

---

[46] Martin A, Rogoff & Edward Collins, Jr., *The Caroline Incident and the Development of International Law,* 16 BROOK. J. INT'L L 493, 494 (1990).
[47] *Id.*
[48] Thomas Nichols, *Address Delivered at Niagara Falls on the Anniversary of the Burning of the Caroline*, MERCURY & BUFFALONIAN EXTRA, Dec. 29, 1838 at 6-7.
[49] Rogoff & Collins, *supra* note 47, at 494.

one thousand men.[50] Almost immediately the rebels employed their increased strength to carry out harassing attacks on both the Canadian mainland and vulnerable British vessels steaming up the Niagara River.[51] Consequently, on December 23, 1837, Sir Francis Head, the Lieutenant Governor of Upper Canada, asked Henry Fox, the British Minister in Washington, to make a formal request that the United States government intervene to stop all pro rebel activity occurring on American soil.[52] Sir Head prodded Minister Fox to speak directly with the federal government because Head's earlier letter addressed to New York Governor William Marcy had gone unanswered.[53] For the purposes of this paper, these harassing attacks may be viewed as analogous to minor cyberattacks against the United States, during which our defenses are probed or code is embedded in out computer systems for future use. They are not major military operations, but they are nonetheless actions taken in contravention of the interests of the United States. An important fact in our analysis is that the "attacks" from the Caroline were clearly being launched from American soil, yet the United States government did nothing to stop them, even after such request was made by the Government of Canada. This construct will become very important as we consider attribution in the cyberattack context.

On December 29, 1837, impatient with the slow pace of diplomacy, Sir Head decided to act unilaterally to protect British interest and Canadian civilians from possible invasion and he summoned the Canadian militia and installed a cannon battery at Chippewa on the

---

[50] R. Y. Jennings, *The Caroline and McLeod Cases,* 32 AM. J. INT'L L. 82, 83 (1938). *See also* Rogoff & Collins, *supra* note 47, at 494.
[51] Jennings, *supra* note 51, at 83.
[52] Rogoff & Collins, *supra* note 47, at 494.
[53] *Id.*

Canadian mainland shore opposite Navy Island.[54] On that day as well, the *Caroline*, a privately owned American steamboat, made three trips to Navy Island conveying men and material to the rebel forces before being docked at Fort Schlosser, in New York State, directly across from Navy Island.[55] Despite the overwhelming evidence that the *Caroline* was ferrying arms and insurgents to Navy Island, there were nonetheless partisan contemporaries who vociferously denied the ship was anything but a civilian transport. As one writer declared in a passage representative of this viewpoint, the *Caroline* "was an American boat and . . . carrying an American flag. She was neither bought, nor chartered, nor hired by any party. . . . Why then should she fear – or wherefore should her crew be armed, or on watch to defend her?"[56]

The opinions of American pundits notwithstanding, upon observing that the *Caroline* was offloading "Stores of War" on Navy Island, Colonel Allan McNab, the commander of the Canadian militia, judged that the *Caroline*'s destruction would serve the double purpose of forestalling reinforcements and supplies from reaching the island as well as deprive the rebels of their means of access to the Canadian mainland.[57] Accordingly, later that night, Colonel McNab ordered Commander Andrew Drew of the Royal Navy to lead fifty-six Canadian militiamen in a clandestine mission to destroy the *Caroline*.[58] However, when Colonel McNab ordered the attack, he mistakenly believed that the *Caroline* was berthed in the British-Canadian territorial waters off Navy Island.[59] When

---

[54] *Id.*
[55] *Id.* at 494-95.
[56] Nichols, *supra* note 49 at 3.
[57] Jennings, *supra* note 51, at 83, 84.
[58] Doyle, *supra* note 45 at 11, 12.
[59] Id. at 12.

Commander Drew discovered the *Caroline* was not at Navy Island, he directed a portion of his men to float downstream in five boats where they found the *Caroline* docked at Fort Schlosser, New York.[60] Ignoring the fact that the ship was moored in American waters, Commander Drew ordered his men to board the vessel and "immediately commenced a warfare with muskets, swords, and cutlasses" upon the crew of the *Caroline*.[61] In the close quarters battle, two Americans were killed and the *Caroline* was "set on fire, cut loose from the dock, was towed into the current of the river, there abandoned, and soon after descended the Niagara falls."[62]

The intrusion of British-Canadian forces into sovereign United States territory and the destruction of the *Caroline* both served to inflame American anger.[63] Additionally, conflicting press reports about the incident spread confusion and fear, which lead to hardened perceptions on both sides of the border. As one American proto yellow journalist declared, the *Caroline* was engaged in harmless trade and was completely surprised by the "murderous attack . . . British officers and British soldiers sprang upon the deck, and mocking at the flag of our county and despising its boast of protection, commenced with insatiate greediness the work of death."[64] Initially, twelve crew members were reported missing and perhaps killed but later

---

[60] *Id.*
[61] Jennings, *supra* note 51, at 84.
[62] *Id.* at 84.
[63] James A. Green, *Docking the Caroline: Understanding the Relevance of the Formula in Contemporary Customary International Law Concerning Self Defense,* 14 CARDOZO J. INT'L & COMP. L. 429, 434 (2006). Indeed, even President Martin Van Buren who maintained a reputation for timidity denounced the incident as an "outrage." *Id.*
[64] Henry Brooke, *Book of Pirates,* 184 (1841).

investigation revealed that two people lost their lives: an African American sailor named Amos Durfee whose body was found on the quay with a musket ball through his head and a cabin boy known as "little Billy" who was shot while attempting to escape the militiamen.[65]

In addition to print media, woodcarvings and at least one dramatic contemporary painting by artist George Tattersall portrayed a sensational image of a burning yet intact *Caroline* hurtling toward the precipice of Niagara Falls amidst swift and powerful white capped waves.[66] The shocking image of a steamboat in conflagration plummeting over Niagara Falls captured the imagination of contemporaries to such an extent that even a decade later journalists dedicated to the truth needed to reiterate that "[i]t is impossible that the notorious Caroline steamer could have reached the great crescent in a state of integrity; these glorious rapids, which come onwards, leaping, roaring and exulting, like an army of hoary giants, must have torn the little craft to shreds as she passed through them."[67]

Although the actual death toll was made eventually made public, the melodramatic reporting drove a jingoistic impulse in both the United States and Canada. In the American press, "witnesses" told gripping tales that people near the river bank could hear the brave but doomed sailors' "wails . . . as they faced a double death" of burning and drowning.[68] Not to be outdone, Canadian patriots penned a "New Song" that lampooned the ironic history of the United States in which white slaveholding colonists decried their lack of

---

[65] Jennings, *supra* note 51, at 84. *See also McLeod's Trial,* THE NEW WORLD, Oct. 9, 1841, at 238.

[66] DEREK HAYES, CANADA: AN ILLUSTRATED HISTORY 129 (2004).

[67] *A Letter From the Falls of Niagara,* BAPTIST MEMORIAL & MONTHLY RECORD, Apr. 1, 1848, at 127.

[68] *Historical Narratives of Early Canada,* available at: http://www.uppercanadahistory.ca/tt/tt6.html.

freedom under the supposed yoke of British tyranny.[69] As the song boasted, when Mackenzie's rebel band was defeated in Ontario "[t]o Buffalo he did retreat and said We used him ill, Sir; The Buffalonians did sympathize And soon began to roar, Sir, They kicked up such a tarnation noise It reached the British shore Sir; . . . No slave shall ever breathe our air, No Lynch Law e'er shall bind us, So keep your Yankee mobs at Home, For Britons still you'll find us."[70]

Although tensions along the border remained elevated in the two years following the incident, diplomatic resolutions were muted.[71] During this period, diplomacy reached only so far as an exchange of letters between British Minister Henry Fox and United States Secretary of State John Forsyth.[72] While Secretary Forsyth demanded "redress" on behalf of the United States, Minister Fox insisted that the "piratical character of the steam boat *Caroline* and the necessity of self-defense and self-preservation, under which Her Majesty's subjects acted in destroying that vessel seem to be sufficiently established."[73] Additionally, Andrew Stevenson, the American Minister to Britain, sent a letter regarding the incident to Lord Palmerston, the British Foreign Secretary, where he argued that because there was no imminent danger to the Canadian militia, Britain could not claim to have acted in self-defense.[74] Much to

---

[69] *Id.*
[70] *Id.*
[71] Green, *supra* note 64 at 434.
[72] *Id.*
[73] *Id.*
[74] *Id.*

the ire of many Americans, Lord Palmerston took more than three years to respond to Stevenson's letter.[75]

Public furor in America over the destruction of the *Caroline* was reignited on November 12, 1840 with the arrest of a Canadian named Alexander McLeod. After McLeod bragged in a tavern of his involvement in the affair, he was arrested by American authorities and charged with both arson and the murder of *Caroline* crewmember Amos Durfee.[76] On December 13, 1840, Minister Fox wrote a letter to Secretary Forsyth denying that McLeod was involved in the incident and calling for his prompt release.[77] Minister Fox further argued that the attack on the *Caroline* was an incident of state action taken in self defense by persons under the authority of superior officers and therefore the United States could not proceed against persons in their individual capacity.[78] In reply, Secretary Forsyth dodged the substance of Fox's argument and merely explained that according to the American system of governance, the matter was within the jurisdiction of the New York trial court rather than the federal executive branch because McLeod was charged with an offense allegedly committed in New York and in violation of New York law.[79]

If Secretary Forsyth, an aged Southern Jacksonian Democrat, was not up to the task of a

---

[75] *Id.* In the interim period before Lord Palmerston answered Stevenson's letter, the American press railed against him as a "rash man, fond of a *coup d'etat*, willing to strike rashly . . . his course in regard to the Caroline steamer will not be forgotten. . . . [W]e may justly fear that he would prefer some sudden movement upon the United States to patient waiting for greater provocation." *Lord Palmerston*, NEW YORK SPECTATOR, Dec. 8, 1841, at 3.
[76] Rogoff & Collins, *supra* note 47, at 495.
[77] *Id.*
[78] *Id.* at 497.
[79] *Id.* at 495.

rigorous intellectual exchange with Minister Fox, his replacement Daniel Webster was a more than qualified opponent. A Phi Beta Kappa graduate of Dartmouth College, Webster was a constitutional lawyer who argued before the United States Supreme Court as well as a former Massachusetts Senator when he replaced Forsyth as Secretary of State on March 4, 1841.[80] Secretary Webster agreed with Minister Fox that McLeod should be released but Governor William Seward of New York, a staunch Whig, refused to issue a *nolle prosequi* to suspend further criminal proceedings.[81] Consequently, McLeod's case went forward until he was eventually acquitted at trial upon proof of an alibi.[82]

Although Secretary Webster's views regarding McLeod dovetailed with those of Minister Fox, he took strong exception to the prevailing British view that the destruction of the *Caroline* was justified as an act of self-defense.[83] In a letter to Minister Fox dated April 24, 1841, Secretary Webster set forth what became known as the *Caroline* doctrine.[84] In Secretary Webster's perspective, use of force by one state against another is permissible as an act of self-defense only if the force applied is both necessary and proportionate. Secretary Webster began his letter with an admonition that the Canadian militiamen's actions could not be justified "by any reasonable application or construction of the right of self defense under the laws of nations."[85] While

---

[80] IRVING H. BARTLETT, DANIEL WEBSTER 3 (1978).
[81] *Domestic Occurrences*, NEW HAMPSHIRE SENTINEL, Jan. 28 1841, at 308.
[82] *Id.*
[83] Rogoff & Collins, *supra* note 47, at 497.
[84] Jane Campbell Moriarty, *"While Dangers Gather": The Bush Preemption Doctrine, Battered Women, Imminence, and Anticipatory Self-Defense*, 30 N.Y.U. REV. L. & SOC. CHANGE 1, 7 (2005).
[85] Daniel Webster, *Case of the Caroline*, NILES' NATIONAL REGISTER, Sept. 24, 1842, at 57.

Secretary Webster admitted a nation's right to self-defense, he emphasized that the extent of this right must be judged on a case by case basis "and when its alleged exercise has led to the commission of hostile acts within the territory of a power at peace, nothing less than a clear and absolute necessity can afford ground of justification."[86] While acknowledging that the immensity of the border between the United States and Canada will likely lead to violence equally against the will of both governments, Secretary Webster underscored that regarding the *Caroline* incident, there was no reason to believe that American citizens committed hostile acts against Canadian interests.[87] After imparting this dubious remark, Secretary Webster then articulated the *Caroline* test whereby a government seeking to employ anticipatory self-defense must demonstrate "a necessity of self defense, instant, overwhelming, leaving no choice of means, and no moment for deliberation."[88] Adding a proportionality element, Secretary Webster went on to state that it will be for the British government to likewise show that "even supposing the necessity of the moment authorized them to enter the territories of the United States at all, [the militiamen] did nothing unreasonable or excessive; since the act justified by the necessity of self-defense, must be limited by that necessity, and kept clearly within it."[89]

The overwhelming majority of international law scholars consider Secretary Webster's *Caroline* test as the seminal definition of what constitutes permissible

---

[86] *Id.* Perhaps not surprisingly, Secretary Webster recalled the 18th century American prohibition against keeping standing armies in times of peace for the reason why the United States might have more trouble controlling its border population than Canada. *Id.*
[87] *Id.*
[88] *Id.*
[89] *Id.* at 58

use of force in anticipation of an attack on a state.[90] Indeed, as Professor Christine Gray remarked in 2000, the *Caroline* test has attained a mythical status not only for its definition of imminence but also for its requirement that the use of force be necessary and proportional to a coming attack.[91] Moreover, as described by British scholar R. Y. Jennings in his highly regarded 1938 article, the *Caroline* test had a humanist element because while it defined the right and left limits of national self-defense, it rescued the concept from "naturalist" notions of an absolute primordial right of self-preservation and thereby became the *locus classicus* of the law of self-defense.[92]

While scholars agree on the importance of the *Caroline* test in discussions of *jus ad bellum*, there is ongoing debate whether the doctrine is a suitable national security policy for the 21st century. In Dr. Michael W. Doyle's provocative recent book, he advanced the thesis that the *Caroline* test is woefully under-inclusive given the current threats to global security. In his view, Secretary Webster's doctrine merely justifies defensive reactions to imminent threats and such a parochial perspective could be disastrous in a thermonuclear age riven by terrorist acts and rogue nation states.[93]

Dr. Doyle opens his book by arguing that the *Caroline* incident is essentially ahistorical because it failed to meet the requirements of self-defense set forth by Secretary Webster and thus never represented the

---

[90] John Yoo, *Using Force,* 71 U. CHI. L. 729, 741 (2004).
[91] *Id. See also* CHRISTINE GRAY, INTERNATIONAL LAW AND THE USE OF FORCE 105 (2000).
[92] Jennings, *supra* note 14, at 192.
[93] Doyle, *supra* note 45, at 15. *See* Dodi-Lee Hect, *Tackling the Crisis of Anticipatory Defense: A First, Second, Third, and Fourth Strike at the Issue,* 47 COLUM. J. TRANSNAT'L L. 648, 648-49 (2009).

standards for which the case has become famous.[94] First, the attack on the *Caroline* was unnecessary because the British-Canadian militiamen enjoyed significant force superiority over the Mackenzie rebels on Navy Island. Second, the American government never intended to attack Canada. And third, there was no immediate threat to the British-Canadian forces.[95] Yet in Dr. Doyle's view, the real fault of the *Caroline* test lies not in its synthetic foundation but rather that the doctrine provides insufficient time for nations to guard their legitimate interests in self-defense when they still have some "choice of means" albeit no peaceful options and some "time to deliberate" among the dangerous choices left at their disposal. Accordingly, he insists that *Caroline* conditions are exceedingly rare in the real world and lists only the Netherlands' declaration of war on Japan as the one example of *Caroline* principles clearly validating an act of preemption.[96] Consequently, Dr. Doyle relegates the *Caroline* test to the status of an instructional cautionary tale that shows the difficulty of drawing a clear line separating imminent preemption from disallowed prevention.[97] The three factors mentioned by Dr. Doyle which he argues render the incident ahistorical are strikingly familiar to how a modern cyberattack may appear. First, the attack on the *Caroline* was unnecessary because the British-Canadian militiamen enjoyed significant force superiority over the Mackenzie rebels on Navy Island—this is almost always the case when one considers the United States as opposed to our enemies, with the possible exceptions of Russia and China. Second, the American government never intended to attack Canada- this goes directly to the

---

[94] Doyle, *supra* note 45, at 14.
[95] *Id.* at 13, 14.
[96] *Id.* at 15.
[97] *Id.* at 15, 16.

issue of attribution, an attack may easily be launched from a country, or routed through a particular country, which was not aware of, or intending for such attack to occur. And third, there was no immediate threat to the British-Canadian forces- this is also generally the case, however, in the realm of cyberattack, it is very difficult to judge what the action threat picture may be at any given moment.

Dr. Doyle further asserts that the potential for widespread carnage posed by weapons of mass destruction (WMDs) is heightened today as opposed to during the Cold War. In that period, the doctrine of mutual assured destruction imposed a nuclear stalemate because the Soviets were rationally deterrable while terrorist cells driven by religious fanaticism and martyrdom are far more difficult to deter.[98] For this reason, the demands of modern asymmetrical warfare necessitates that preventive responses that entail unilateral armed attack or multilateral enforcement measures remain lawful.[99] I would argue that the assertions of Dr. Doyle as related to concerns about WMDs are, at least conceptually, valid in the cyberattack arena, the ultimate in asymmetric warfare, as well.

If the *Caroline* case established the 19th century Anglo-American concept of national anticipatory self-defense, the United States reaffirmed its right ninety-one years later when it joined the Kellogg-Briand Pact.[100] Therefore, by the time the United States began negations to replace the League of Nations with a more dynamic international organization in the later stages of World

---

[98] *Id.* at 23, 24.
[99] *Id.* at 20.
[100] Amy E. Eckert & Manooher Mofidi, *Doctrine or Doctrinaire – The First Strike Doctrine and Preemptive Self-Defense Under International Law,* 12 TUL. J. INT'L & COMP. L. 117, 130 (2004).

War II, anticipatory self-defense was an accepted principle of international law.[101] As discussed above, pursuant to Article 51 of the United Nations (UN) Charter, "[n]othing in the present Charter shall impair the inherent right of individual or collective self-defense if an armed attack occurs against a Member of the United Nations, until the Security Council has taken measures necessary to maintain international peace and security."[102]

Perhaps not surprisingly given the tenuous nature of global stability, Article 51 is the subject of continuing debate in the post 9/11 world. Unlike in the *Caroline* test, anticipatory self-defense is lawful under Article 51 only "if an armed attack occurs" and scholars are divided whether that phrase limits the right of self-defense such that it could properly be exercised by a victim state only in the wake of an attack.[103] Broadly speaking, the disputants of this question can be separated into two groups: the strict constructionists and the liberal constructionists.[104] The strict constructionists assert that Article 51 is constrained by a plain reading of the language and that the customary right to self-defense is safeguarded only in the situation of a prior armed attack.[105] Prominent strict constructionists such as Professor Ian Brownlie argue that if the UN Charter restrictions on the use of force were loosened, it would be impossible to determine whether a nation honestly resorted to their right of self-defense or merely invoked Article 51 to conceal their aggressive intentions toward

---

[101] *Id.*
[102] Keith A. Petty, *Criminalizing Force: Resolving the Threshold Question for the Crime of Aggression in the Context of Modern Conflict*, 33 SEATTLE U. L. REV. 105, 115 (2009).
[103] *Id.* at 137.
[104] *Id.*
[105] *Id.*

other states.[106] By contrast, the liberal constructionists posit that Article 51 should be construed in light of customary international law and that assuming the requirements of necessity, proportionality, and imminence are met, the right of self-defense allows the unilateral use of force in anticipation of an armed attack.[107] From this perspective, the Bush Doctrine was not the progenitor of the United States' preemption policy. Indeed, to take the most commonly cited example, President Kennedy's 1962 decision to forestall Soviet installation of short and intermediate ballistic missiles in Cuba by declaring a "quarantine" of the island stands as the most prominent example of American strategic preemption.[108]

Further complicating the debate between the strict and liberal constructionists is that the UN Charter procedures for regulating the use of force were never applied uniformly during the Cold War. First, due to their permanent seats on the Security Council, the United States and the Soviet Union could veto any effort to authorize force than ran counter to their national interests.[109] Second, warfare in the 20th century changed the calculus regarding the question of imminence because innovations in technology such as thermonuclear intercontinental ballistic missiles allowed an opponent to acquire a decisive advantage if allowed to strike first.[110] Third, the legitimate concern for humanitarian intervention defined as the use of force in the internal affairs of a nation to prevent large-scale deprivation of human rights imperils reading Articles 2

---

[106] Yoo, *supra* note 92, at 738-39.
[107] Eckert & Mofidi, *supra* note 102, at 137.
[108] David B. Rivkin, *The Virtues of Preemptive Deterrence*, 29 HARV. J. L. & PUB. POL'Y 85, 86 (2005).
[109] Yoo, *supra* note 92, at 742.
[110] *Id.* at 743.

(4) and 51 as anything but a prohibition on the use of force by states for any reason other than self-defense.[111]

As Dr. Doyle explains in *Striking First*, the Bush Doctrine emerged as a foil to both the *Caroline* test and Article 51 of the UN Charter. On September 12, 2002, President Bush addressed the UN and refocused international attention on the principles of preemptive self-defense and whether the United States should rely on this doctrine as a justification for the unilateral use of force.[112] As articulated, the Bush Doctrine was designed to prevent America's enemies from threatening the United States or its allies with WMDs.[113] Furthermore, the Bush Doctrine claimed the legal right to take military action to preempt gathering threats to United States national security with or without the sanction of the UN Security Council.[114] Additionally, President Bush asserted that the United States must remain proactive to prevent rogue nations that may harbor or assist terrorists from ever acquiring WMDs.[115] Consequently, a number of scholars believe that the Bush Doctrine re-cast anticipatory self-defense into an entitlement of preemption based on a different understanding of imminence where America "must adapt the concept of

---

[111] *Id.* For instance, the tragic case of Rwanda during the 1990s is but one example where a relatively minor intervention by the great powers might have prevented genocide. *Id.* at 744.

[112] Martinez, *supra* note 3, at 123.

[113] Tomasz Iwanek, *The 2003 Invasion of Iraq: How the System Failed*, 15 J. CONFLICT & SECURITY 89, 113 (2010).

[114] David B. Rivkin, et al., *Preemption and Law in the Twenty-First Century*, 5 CHI. J. INT'L L. 467, 467 (2005).

[115] Gregory E. Maggs, *How the United States Might Justify A Preemptive Strike On A Rogue Nation's Nuclear Weapon Development Facilities Under The U.N. Charter*, 57 SYRACUSE L. REV. 465, 469 (2007).

imminent threat to the capabilities of today's adversaries."[116]

To gain insight into the Bush Doctrine, certain legal scholars have turned to the past and examined the work of eminent 18th century international law theorist Emmerich de Vattel who perceived anticipatory self-defense as a fundamental legal right held by states and individuals alike.[117] Vattel's famous example is illustrative of the intellectual calculus behind the Bush Doctrine: "[o]n occasion, where it is impossible, or too dangerous to wait for absolute certainty, we may justly act on a reasonable presumption. If a stranger presents his piece at me in a wood, I am not yet certain that he intends to kill me; but shall I, in order to be convinced of his design, allow him to fire? What reasonable casuist will deny me the right of preventing him?"[118]

To be sure, Vattel's historical purpose was to justify military action against the French monarch but his exposition regarding preemptive self-defense is cited by Bush Doctrine supporters to illustrate their contention that preemptive self-defense is grounded in customary international law.[119] To further bolster their arguments, Bush Doctrine proponents look toward iconic World War II history. As the argument goes, Britain and France used their right to preemptive self defense to warn Nazi Germany that an invasion of Poland would be construed as a *casas belli*. At the time, Germany's military was not directly menacing either Britain or France especially in light of British Prime Minister

---

[116] Major John J. Merriam, *Natural Law and Self-Defense,* 206 MIL. L. REV. 43, 69 (2010).
[117] Rivkin, *supra* note 116, at 468.
[118] *Id.*
[119] *Id.* See also Michael J. Glennon, *Military Action against Terrorists under International Law: The Fog of Law, Self-Defense, Inherence, and Incoherence in Article 51 of the United Nations Charter,* 25 HARV. J. L. & PUB. POL'Y 539, N. 62 (2002).

Neville Chamberlain's infamous pronouncement of "peace for our time" with Hitler and the only lawful means either nation had to issue its ultimatum to Germany was grounded in their right to anticipate future attacks.[120]

Yet scholars who take exception to the Bush Doctrine correctly point out that it obviates the Enlightenment notion of the rule of law that the state may generally employ harsh measures only on the basis of past wrongdoing that has been established to a high degree of certainty by a fundamentally fair process.[121] As Professor David Cole argues, the preventive paradigm rejects the rule of law's presumption against employing coercive force on the basis of conjecture regarding unpredictable future events.[122] Moreover, President Bush's concern that "[i]f we wait for threats to fully materialize, we will have waited too long" is a double-edged sword that can have disastrous consequences. In Professor Cole's view, while the preventive impulse may be salutary, it risks not only grievous errors but also erodes the respect that the rule of law offers to "regimes that play by the rules."[123] Furthermore, to the extent that the 2003 Iraq War is regarded as an act of preemptive self-defense, the difficult aftermath of that intervention may presage an era where nations resist resorting to large-scale preemptive self-defense. After all, the Iraq War highlighted the considerable policy difficulties that arise with unilateral preemptive action: an inability to attract allies, the dangers of faulty intelligence regarding a foreign state's weapons program and relations with

---

[120] Rivkin, *supra* note 116, at 470.
[121] DAVID COLE & JULES LOBEL, LESS SAFE, LESS FREE: WHY AMERICA IS LOSING THE WAR ON TERROR, 33 (2007).
[122] *Id.* at 34.
[123] *Id.*

terrorist groups, the political, economic, and human costs in pursuing elective wars, and the resistance level of radicalized factions to what is viewed by them as an unwarranted foreign invasion.[124]

In Dr. Doyle's perspective, the *Caroline* test is a relic of an age before WMDs while the Bush Doctrine is appallingly over-inclusive to the point where if it were adopted globally today "it could open the door to wars between Pakistan and India and perhaps even China and Taiwan."[125] Moreover, because the Bush Doctrine disregarded any pretense of an imminence requirement, it promulgated a subjective and open-ended standard that invites chaos because "every state will be preempting every other state's preventative strikes."[126] In his dissatisfaction with both the *Caroline* test and the Bush Doctrine, Dr. Doyle locates the UN and its Security Council in particular as the quintessential middle ground between two extremes. After all, reasons Dr. Doyle, pursuant to Article 39, the UN Security Council shall "determine the existence of *any* threat to the peace, breach of the peace or act of aggression" and take whatever action, including coercive embargoes and forcible measures by land, air, or sea, that the Security Council sees fit.[127] Acknowledging *realpolitik*, Dr. Doyle explains Article 39 contains two unresolved problems: first, the Security Council has failed to authorize force when it was arguably justified; and second, there is a dearth of adequate standards to guide the Security Council's deliberations.[128]

In his second essay, Dr. Doyle proposes a solution for the inherent lack of standards dilemma

---

[124] Sean Murphy, *The Doctrine of Preemptive Self-Defense*, 50 VILL. L. REV. 699, 747 (2005).
[125] *Id.* at 28. *See also* Hect, *supra* note 95, at 652.
[126] Doyle, *supra* note 45, at 26.
[127] *Id.* at 30 (emphasis in original).
[128] *Id.* at 33.

found in Article 39. Similar to the four pronged test espoused by Secretary Webster, Dr. Doyle argues the Security Council should be guided by the four elements of lethality, likelihood, legitimacy, and legality to gauge the seriousness of threats not yet imminent and the appropriate responses to them.[129] While three of the standards are perhaps conceptually straightforward, the legitimacy prong itself includes three elements: (1) weighing proportionately the threatened harm against the likely benefit-cost of the response; (2) limiting the response to the minimum necessary to effectively deal with the threat; and (3) seeking the relevant deliberation.[130] Applying these standards, Dr. Doyle argues that any nation considering anticipatory force should attain prior approval from the Security Council and that each voting member must state in public its reasons for accepting or rejecting the application to authorize prevention.[131] However, given the unpredictable record of the Security Council's decisions, if the vote is negative, individual nations could form a national commission to examine the facts before sending its report to the Security Council for an international investigation.[132] In the end, Dr. Doyle's expresses his remarkable if not altogether practical or convincing methodology in terms of a specific multiplicative equation where Justified Prevention = Lethality x Likelihood x Legitimacy x Legality.[133]

VI. Applying the *Caroline* Doctrine to Cyberattack in the 21st Century

Addressing a joint session of Congress on December 7, 1841 President John Tyler remarked on the

---

[129] *Id.* at 46.
[130] *Id.* at 57.
[131] *Id.* at 61.
[132] Doyle, *supra* note 45, at 62.
[133] *Id.* at 63.

Caroline incident and essentially repudiated what would become the Bush Doctrine. In the chaotic days following 9/11, Vice President Cheney espoused the "One Percent Doctrine" wherein if there is a one percent chance of a serious threat materializing, policymakers must perceive that threat as an event certain to occur.[134] Additionally, coupling Vice President Cheney's viewpoint with former Secretary of Defense Donald Rumsfeld's admission that "the absence of evidence is not evidence of absence" meant that a scintilla of evidence became a high probability and even situations where there is no evidence of even a one percent probability, that is not sufficient proof for the absence of sufficient provocation to warrant a preemptive attack with overwhelming force.[135] In direct contrast to the views expressed by members of the Bush Administration, President Tyler, calling upon her Majesty's government to apologize for burning the *Caroline*, steadfastly refused to sanction the right of any nation to engage in preemption action without sufficient provocation. In his understanding, to recognize preemption as "an admissible practice that each government . . . may take vengeance into its own hands . . . and in the absence of any pressing or overruling necessity, may invade the territory of the other, would inevitably lead to results equally deplored by both."[136]

In his comment on Dr. Doyle's essays, Dean Koh argues for a per se ban on unilateral anticipatory attack.[137] Dean Koh's position is admirable and humane and would that a world existed that a ban on anticipatory self-defense made the need for unilateral action obsolete.

---

[134] *Id.* at 107.
[135] *Id.*
[136] *President's Message to the Senate and House of Representatives of the United States,* ALEXANDRIA GAZETTE, Dec. 7, 1841, at 3.
[137] Doyle, *supra* note 45, at 107.

As it stands, Dean Koh is correct that Dr. Doyle's "Four Ls" of lethality, likelihood, legitimacy, and legality and their subparts is a complex test that would be difficult for bureaucracies to apply consistently.[138] On the other hand, there is a valid argument that Dean Koh is incorrect to take exception to the idea that in certain instances where the Security Council is paralyzed by indecision or political infighting, states have the discretion to take anticipatory unilateral action. The problem is that whereas Dean Koh is too hesitant to employ anticipatory self-defense, Dr. Doyle is both too eager to expand the parameters of the *Caroline* doctrine and overly reliant on the Security Council as an adequate response to the current challenges of WMDs, rogue states, and terrorism.

Despite the potential applicability of the *Caroline* test to the security exigencies of the 21st century, certain modifications are necessary to update Secretary Webster's test for an age in which cyberattacks can crisscross the world on the internet at the push of a button. The *Caroline* test distinguishes itself from the results of Bush Doctrine preemption measures because it curtails the right to national self-defense to situations where there is a real threat, the response is essential and proportional and all peaceful means of resolving the dispute were exhausted.[139] To be sure, Dean Koh's admonition regarding the difficulty of applying legal tests to real world instances is acknowledged but so too is the realization that it is likewise folly to make perfect the enemy of the good.[140]

---

[138] *Id.* at 101, 112.

[139] Amos N. Guiora, *Anticipatory Self-Defense and International Law – A Re-Evaluation,* 13 J. Conflict & Security L. 3, 8-9 (2008).

[140] Jide Nzelibe & John Yoo, *Rational War and Constitutional Design,* 115 YALE L. J. 2512, 2541 (2006)

Converting Secretary Webster's language into a modern legal test, an anticipatory strike must be (1) overwhelming in its necessity; (2) leaving no choice of means; (3) facing so imminent a threat that there is no moment for deliberation; and (4) proportional.[141] Consequently, a plain reading of the test implicates the liberal constructionist interpretation of Article 51 of the UN Charter that the right to self-defense entails a lawful use of force in anticipation of an armed attack. Therefore, given the current threats to global security, the "necessity" prong is the critical element of the *Caroline* tests that requires modernization. As Secretary Webster explained, the necessity prong is informed by the proportionality element because America "does not wish to disturb the tranquility of the world. . . . It is jealous of its rights . . . most especially, of the right of the absolute immunity of its territory, against aggression from abroad . . . while it will at the same time, as scrupulously, refrain from infringing on the rights of others."[142]

Recently, Professor Amos Guiora proposed using a "strict scrutiny" approach to self-defense against non-state actors wherein the executive would convince a court based on relevant, reliable, and corroborated intelligence that an anticipatory strike is appropriate.[143] Yet because the concept of employing a strict scrutiny standard for intelligence evaluation is fundamentally sound, the American government should extend it to include state actors as well. The logistics are perhaps less daunting than may first appear and involve two steps. First, the executive submits reliable intelligence information to a court of law. Second, the court examines the intelligence and subsequently rules as to

---

[141] Doyle, *supra* note 45, at 12, 13.
[142] Webster, *supra* note 87, at 58.
[143] See Guiora, *supra* note 142, at 16.

whether the information is sufficiently probative to warrant some form of anticipatory self-defense.[144] Importantly, this tribunal should be a creature of statute similar to the FISA court and thereby provide a means for the legislature to provide an additional check on both the executive and judicial branches. Moreover, unlike Professor Guiora's model, this proposal is not calling for an overwhelming change in the nature of the relationship between the executive and judicial branches because the executive would retain the power to veto the court's opinion or take direct action should for example an emergency situation involving WMDs occur.[145] This model, while solid in concept, is very problematic unless we are able to develop the appropriate means to attribute cyberattacks to particular actors. Or, in the alternative, are able to attribute the attacks to particular networks under within the territorial jurisdiction of nation states. If this becomes possible, with a high degree of accuracy, then we would be able to make reasonable requests that these nations restrict the activity going on within their borders. Given the fact that the internet is not generally restricted by territorial jurisdiction, we would have to greatly enhance cooperation between nations as well as fund international policing agencies such as Interpol.

Significantly, this model is not intended to be a perfect solution where if followed resulting history would show that the American government never undertook anticipatory self-defense action without sufficient provocation. A second acknowledged deficiency is that the model is specifically designed for the American system of governance and therefore cannot be transferred wholesale internationally. Nonetheless, because a single solution cannot solve every problem that is no reason to ignore the model's potential for

---

[144] *Id.* at 23, 24.
[145] *Id.* at 23.

positively influencing when and how the United States protects its citizenry. Instead, this schema is meant to safeguard the American government from reflexively taking potentially disastrous actions in the name of anticipatory self-defense. Essentially, this model provides a pressure valve designed to minimize the tragic results of mistaken intelligence or an unnecessary rush to armed conflict. In other words, the court would provide a moment of repose and deliberation where the executive could present its best arguments for the use of force and benefit from the insight contained in the court's opinion. In doing so, the court would act like an American Security Council without potentially sacrificing the safety of American citizens upon the interested decisions of the nations comprising the UN. As Dr. Doyle correctly states "in the world we live in today, where . . . the discretion of leaders is rightly suspect, we as citizens need to propose the standards that our leaders should employ when they claim to protect us."[146] Yet despite the laudable standards contained in Article 51, the UN is too haphazard a body to be given the ultimate responsibility of protecting Americans. In significant part, therefore, the answer to enhancing peace and security throughout the world lies within.

Looking ahead into the 21st century, it is likely that all manner of threats will continue, including cyberattack. As globalization, radicalism, and technological advances continue to change the means and nature of warfare, the United States requires bright-line rules regarding its use of anticipatory self-defense in the cyber context. Provided the current range of threats and uncertainties, it is unwise for America to look entirely to the interested UN to safeguard its citizenry. Similarly, given the disastrous consequences of preemption, the United States government should

---

[146] Doyle, *supra* note 45, at 159.

employ methods designed to assist the executive make reasoned and proportional responses. As modified by strict scrutiny analysis, the *Caroline* test is not expansive, obviates preemption but not anticipatory self-defense and is not overly reliant on the UN. Consequently, the updated *Caroline* doctrine may provide a flexible standard to meet the challenges of the coming decades provided the forensic ability to analyze the origin of attacks keeps pace with the technology allowing the attacks to occur.

Cyber Redux: The Schmitt Analysis, Tallinn Manual and US Cyber Policy

By James E. McGhee*

I. INTRODUCTION

Cyber law and policy are all the rage these days. Both are mentioned almost daily in the news. It is reported that China, Russia, Iran and North Korea are bombarding the US with cyber intrusions, both to the DoD networks as well as private networks.[1] Additionally, hacktivist groups like Anonymous and LulzSec are becoming household names. In addition, focused cyber threats have resulted in exposed intellectual property, research and development, military plans, proprietary information and extortion. For instance, when Coca-Cola was negotiating what would have been the largest foreign purchase of a Chinese company; Chinese hackers were inside the Coca-Cola network and were able to obtain details about the negotiations.[2] Needless to say, Coca-Cola did not make the purchase.

---

* Mr. McGhee is an operational cyber law attorney with the 24th Air Force, Joint Base San Antonio, Lackland AFB. The views expressed in this Article are those of the author in his personal capacity and do not necessarily represent those of the US Air Force or any other US governmental entity.

[1] Todd Beamon, *Rep. Rogers: China and Russia Conduct 'Vicious' Cyberattacks on U.S.*, NEWSMAX, (May 28, 2013), http://www.newsmax.com/newsfront/rogers-china-russia-cyberattacks/2013/05/28/id/506756.

[2] David E. Sanger, David Barboza & Nicole Perlroth, *Chinese Army Unit is Seen as Tied to Hacking Against U.S.*, NEW YORK TIMES

More recently it has been discovered that state actors have been going beyond mere theft and espionage. Now, they are worming their way into more sensitive networks. Iran has engaged in several high-profile distributed denial of service "attacks" on some of the nation's largest financial institutions. Recently, the Wall Street Journal reported that, "Iranian-backed hackers have escalated a campaign of cyberassaults against U.S. corporations by launching infiltration and surveillance missions against the computer networks running energy companies."[3] This type of activity represents a striking escalation from simply stealing.

Cyber issues have also seized the attention of Congress and the White House. For several years now there has been an attempt to pass some form of cyber-legislation aimed at protecting the United States from cyber-intrusions. The most recent was executive order 13636, Improving Critical Infrastructure Cyber-security, which tasked the National Institute of Standards and Technology (NIST) to develop a voluntary framework for reducing cyber-security risks to critical infrastructure.[4] It aims to promote voluntary information sharing between the government and those private industries responsible for the nation's critical infrastructure. If nothing else, it is a step in the right direction. Other than that, nothing substantive has been passed by Congress or is likely to be passed in the near future.

(February 18, 2013), *available at:* http://www.nytimes.com/2013/02/19/technology/chinas-army-is-seen-as-tied-to-hacking-against-us.html?pagewanted=1&hp.

[3] Siobhan Gorman & Danny Yadron, *Iran Hacks Energy Firms, U.S. Says,* WALL STREET JOURNAL, May 24, 2013, at 4.

[4] Exec. Order No. 13,636, 78 Fed. Reg. 11,739 (Feb. 12, 2013), *available at*: www.whitehouse.gov/the-press-office/2013/02/12/executive-order-improving-critical-infrastructure-cybersecurity.

One of the continuing problems with cyber or dealing with cyber intrusions is the lack of uniformity in concepts, definitions, rules, policy, and law. In many instances, not only is uniformity lacking, but there is simply a void. While the NIST framework may provide uniformity, it is solely focused on critical infrastructure and therefore does not apply to the vast majority of businesses suffering intrusions. This leaves individual states to determine their own concepts, definitions, rules, policy and law regarding cyber. Moreover, cyber is still too new for customary international law to have developed. If we consider Moonlight Maze to be the first major state-on-state cyber incident, then there have only been about fourteen years for such customary law to develop.[5] The length of time to develop customary international law can vary greatly, but generally takes a significant number of years. The customary law of war has developed over thousands of years, but the practice of limiting conflict evolved primarily in the last 150 years. As a result, there is no general international consensus on how to treat cyber and cyber intrusions. Attempts have been made, however, to create concepts, definitions, rules, policy and law regarding cyber. Some have, to a limited extent, proven useful; others, less so.

One of the main problems with these attempts is that they tend to equate cyber and kinetic strikes as being on the same footing. In other words, they tend to treat them exactly the same. As demonstrated below, this does not always result in clean and easy answers and sometimes leads to absurd results. These attempts also tend to focus on actual cyber-attacks, necessitating inquiry into use of force, armed attack, the United Nations (UN) Charter and the Law of War/Law of Armed Conflict. At this level, the answers are relatively

---

[5] Moonlight Maze (1998-2001), probed government and academic computer systems in the United States.

easy, because the US already abides by those rules. The trickier area lies in the realm below use of force, specifically, cyber-espionage. Keeping in mind that there is no international law proscription against cyber-espionage, the question becomes: *can it ever rise to such a level that it threatens our national security? If so, how is it measured? What is it measured against? Who decides?* Finally, *can victims then respond accordingly or do they have to seek assistance from the proper government authorities? Is it self-defense or hacking back?*

This paper explores three such attempts and discusses the interplay between the Schmitt Analysis, Tallinn Manual and US cyber policy. It attempts to answer whether the Schmitt Analysis remains current and relevant, whether the Tallinn Manual offers anything substantive or new and whether US cyber policy is moving in the right direction. The next section briefly introduces the Schmitt Analysis, the Tallinn Manual and U.S. cyber policy. The subsequent section delves into a more detailed and nuanced discussion of each. The last compares and contrasts all three.

II. BACKGROUND

The Schmitt Analysis was first published in 1999 by Michael Schmitt.[6] In that seminal work, Professor Schmitt identified a number of factors that would likely influence assessments by states as to whether particular cyber operations amounted to a use of force. Professor Schmitt was prescient in tackling the tough cyber questions in the previous century, over thirteen years ago. In 2011, Professor Schmitt published

---

[6] Professor Schmitt, J.D., L.L.M, D.Litt., is Chairman of and Professor at the Department of Law, United States Naval War College. Professor Schmitt is also Honorary Professor at Durham University in the United Kingdom and former Dean of the Marshall Center in Germany.

another article, discussing three questions pertinent to international law governing cyber operations.[7] In that work, he reiterates the factors first identified by him in 1999 as still being relevant to today's discussion regarding international law and cyber. In addition, Professor Schmitt also served as Director of the NATO Cooperative Cyber Defense Centre of Excellence's Tallinn Manual project from 2009 through 2012. The Tallinn Manual was published in early 2013.[8]

The Tallinn Manual consists of "rules" adopted unanimously by an International Group of Experts that are meant to reflect customary international law. Lately much has been heard about the Tallinn Manual in mainstream media as well as military channels. It is touted as a great breakthrough in the quest for international cyber law; the go-to reference for all nations. The common desire is for something in writing delineating international law as it applies to cyber warfare. It offers ninety-five (95) rules for the international use of cyber capabilities. The hoped for goal is a product nations can use to fashion their own legal parameters for international cyber activities. The Tallinn Manual is firmly rooted in the twentieth century development of the law of war (outside the United States more commonly referred to as International Humanitarian Law).

US policy regarding cyber can be traced to the early twentieth century. In a 1918 Joint Resolution, Congress authorized the President to assume control of any telegraph system in the United States and operate it as needed for the duration of World War I. The Communications Act of 1934 formed the Federal

---

[7] Michael N. Schmitt, *Cyber Operations and the Jus Ad Bellum*, 56 VILLANOVA L. REV. 569 (2011).
[8] The Tallinn Manual is available at: https://www.ccdcoe.org/249.html.

Communications Commission (FCC) from the Federal Radio Commission and established a broad regulatory framework for all communications, by wire and radio, that has influenced the development of these technologies ever since. The Brooks Act of 1965 gave the National Bureau of Standards (NBS)—now the Department of Commerce's National Institute of Standards and Technology (NIST)—responsibilities for developing automatic data processing standards and guidelines pertaining to federal computer systems. In 1984, Executive Order 12472 re-chartered the National Communication System (NCS) as those telecommunication assets owned or leased by the Federal government that can meet U.S. national security and emergency preparedness needs. The Department of Homeland Security inherited the NCS in 2003. In 1994, through the Foreign Relations Authorization Act, the Department of State was delegated authority over foreign policy related to international communication and information policy.[9] Presidential Decision Directive 63 (PDD-63), signed in May 1998, established a structure under White House leadership to coordinate the activities of designated lead departments and agencies, in partnership with their counterparts from the private sector, to "eliminate any significant vulnerability to both physical and cyber-attacks on our critical infrastructures, including especially our cyber systems."[10] This policy was updated in 2003 with The National Strategy to Secure Cyberspace. It was further augmented later that year in Homeland Security Presidential Directive 7

---

[9] *See* CYBERSPACE POLICY REVIEW: ASSURING A TRUSTED AND RESILIENT INFORMATION AND COMMUNICATIONS INFRASTRUCTURE 2 (2009), *available* *at:* http://www.whitehouse.gov/assets/documents/Cyberspace_Policy_Review_final.pdf.

[10] William J. Clinton, Presidential Decision Directive 63/NSC-63 (May 22, 1998) at section II.

(HSPD-7), which assigned the Secretary of Homeland Security the responsibility for coordinating the nation's overall critical infrastructure protection efforts, including for cyber infrastructure, across all sectors working in cooperation with designated sector-specific agencies within the Executive Branch.[11] There have been many more updates and supplements and new Presidential Policy Directives as well as HSPDs. These strategies and policies are, by their nature, very broad and thus lacking in actionable directive authority.

III. SCHMITT ANALYSIS

The Schmitt Analysis consists of seven criteria to consider when determining whether a cyber incident/intrusion qualifies as either a use of force or armed attack under the United Nations Charter. First the criteria will be examined as enumerated and explained by Professor Schmitt. Next the factors will be considered in the current e-context in order to determine whether they still offer a useful method to characterize current and emerging cyber threats.

The first is severity, which Professor Schmitt suggests is the most important. The severity of an incident is determined by the harm or damage to individuals and property. Obviously, the more severe the consequences, the more likely the incident/intrusion will be seen as a use of force or armed attack. Those generating only minor inconveniences or irritation will never be so.[12] According to Professor Schmitt, "the more consequences impinge on critical national interests, the more they will contribute to the depiction of a cyber operation as a use of force. In this regard, the scale, scope, and duration of the consequences will have great bearing on the appraisal of their severity."[13]

---

[11] *Supra* n. 9.
[12] Schmitt, *supra* n. 7.
[13] *Id.*

The second criterion is immediacy. "The sooner consequences manifest, the less opportunity states have to seek peaceful accommodation of a dispute or to otherwise forestall their harmful effects. Therefore, states harbor a greater concern about immediate consequences than those that are delayed or build slowly over time."[14]

The third criterion is directness. The greater the attenuation between the initial act and the resulting consequences, the less likely states will be to deem the actor responsible for violating the prohibition on the use of force. Directness examines the chain of causation between the initial incident/intrusion and the resulting consequences. The consequences can either be direct or indirect, depending on the nature of the incident/intrusion.

The fourth criterion is invasiveness. This criterion regards the degree to which a system is penetrated. "The more secure a targeted system, the greater the concern as to its penetration."[15] Thus, a secure system, such as SCADA systems or classified networks, which is penetrated, is far more invasive than an unclassified public network.

The fifth criterion is measurability. "The more quantifiable and identifiable a set of consequences, the more a state's interest will be deemed to have been affected."[16] In other words, what is the measure of damage done as a result of the consequences? Can we put numbers on the cost or the dead or the amount of property damaged or destroyed?

The sixth criterion is presumptive legitimacy. Acts which are not forbidden are permitted; absent an

---

[14] *Id.*
[15] *Id.*
[16] *Id.*

express prohibition, an act is presumptively legitimate.[17] Therefore, those things that are strictly prohibited would tend more towards a use of force or armed attack, whereas those things that are not strictly prohibited would tend not to be.

The seventh and final criterion is responsibility. "The law of state responsibility governs when a state will be responsible for cyber operations. Responsibility lies along a continuum from operations conducted by a state itself to those in which it is merely involved in some fashion. The closer the nexus between a state and the operations, the more likely other states will be inclined to characterize them as uses of force, for the greater the risk posed to international stability."[18]

Examining these factors in light of the current cyber threat environment, *how does one determine the severity of a cyber incident/intrusion if the sole concern is harm or damage done to either property or individuals?* Particularly, if the cyber event does not create similar effects that a kinetic strike would create? One of the key problems with insisting on using old rules, criteria and policies is that, on one hand they attempt to equate cyber events with kinetic events. For example, if a cyber event and a kinetic event both cause the same amount of harm or damage to either property or individuals, it is conceptually easy to claim that they should be treated the same. The rules apply in the same manner. To be sure, Professor Schmitt has stated, "Accordingly, cyber operations that directly result (or are likely to result) in physical harm to individuals or tangible objects equate to armed force, and are therefore uses of force."[19] On the other hand, cyber can create the same overall effects without causing lasting physical

---

[17] *Id.*
[18] Schmitt, *supra* n. 7.
[19] *Id.*

damage or damage at all. For instance, if a cyber event and a kinetic strike both take out a power grid, plunging an area into darkness; the overall effect is the same. However, the kinetic strike would necessarily cause harm and damage to property and likely to individuals as well. By comparison the cyber event would not necessarily cause any physical harm or lasting damage at all. Moreover, the cyber event may very well be reversible. Thus, two events that cause the exact same consequence would, in fact, be treated differently under the old rules and, I submit, the Schmitt Analysis. Under the latter example, there is no physical harm or lasting damage and therefore, under the severity criterion, no use of force and certainly not an armed attack.

The next criterion is immediacy. With a cyber event, the intended effects may not become apparent for days, weeks or even months, as occurred with Stuxnet. A kinetic strike usually produces an instantaneous effect. A key question, therefore, is, when does the cyber event actually take place? Is it the point of insertion or the moment of "attack?" If we apply existing standards I believe Professor Schmitt would answer that the actionable event occurred at the moment of attack. Professor Schmitt has stated, "the introduction into a state's cyber systems of vulnerabilities that are capable of destructive activation at some later date would not constitute a threat of the use of force unless their presence is known to the target state and the originating state exploits them for some coercive purpose."[20] To be fair, he qualifies his statement by suggesting that a threat must be communicated in order to qualify under the UN Charter. I don't necessarily disagree from a technical, legal point of view. That, however, simply begs the question, what constitutes a communication? Doesn't the act of introducing destructive vulnerabilities

---

[20] *Id.*

designed for subsequent activation into another country's systems constitute a threat? Isn't the threat communicated by the mere insertion? If not, and we have to wait for the activation of such "devices", then when does the clock start for determining whether the effects are of immediate concern? If we look at Stuxnet, the "attack" consisted of at least three waves over 10 months and, took time to evolve.[21] The initial insertion into Iranian systems, however, was months, and perhaps even years earlier. Can semi-autonomous delayed effect cyber capabilities register on the immediacy criterion continuum for meeting use of force or armed attack?

To add further confusion into the mix, Professor Schmitt's statement above, "likely to result" seems to be in contradiction to his other statement, "capable of destructive activation at some later date." If the destructive capability is known, then doesn't that fall within the "likely to result" category even without an overt communication from the adversary? If so, doesn't that qualify as a use of force? Let's look at a non-cyber example to illustrate the point. Assume a situation in which a criminal places a bomb in a house. The person is aware of, but unable to remove it and the bomb can be remotely activated. The criminal makes no overt threat to the family. Is this nonetheless a threat to the family? Clearly, the answer is yes. How is the introduction of a cyber vulnerability into control systems different? Is not the threat inferred?

The next criterion is directness. Here the cause and effect in the chain of causation needs to be understood. With kinetic strikes, the cause and effect are intimately related—the strike directly causes the damage or destruction. With cyber, the effects can be very indirect and attenuated. Cyber events may have third or fourth order effects that cause the measurable harm or

---

[21] Falliere et al., W32.Stuxnet Dossier (Symantec, February 2011).

damage. Furthermore, cyber capabilities may have the ability to hide the cause or make it appear as if another cause is to blame. By examining the power grid shut-down by a cyber event further, assume that the perpetrator of the event was sophisticated enough to make it appear as if the shut-down was simply the result of either faulty equipment or operator error or even an act of God—lightning strike. Thus, the ultimate cause is extremely difficult or even impossible to discern. Most serious cyber events will be sophisticated enough to either hide the cause or shift the blame. If not, attempting to trace back the entire causal chain from second, third, fourth order effects and beyond may prove too difficult and time consuming to allow response within a reasonable window. Realize that simply because something is difficult it does not mean it is unworkable. However, when time is of the essence and with cyber it always is, the difficulty and timeliness of making a determination is a paramount concern. How far can this go down the rabbit hole before the subsequent effects are deemed too remote and too indirect? Would all of the subsequent victims be Mrs. Palsgraf?[22]

The next criterion is invasiveness. Here the concern is with the security of the system penetrated and the depth of insertion by the adversaries. For instance, an intrusion into the public-facing website of a major bank is not nearly as invasive as a root-level intrusion into their internal network. Many of our financial institutions have recently been bombarded with DDoS (Distributed Denial of Service) events, which many

---

[22] *Palsgraf v. Long Island Railroad Co.*, 248 N.Y. 339, 162 N.E. 99 (N.Y. 1928) is a seminal case in tort law, establishing the concept of proximate cause and foreseeability, limiting liability to the consequences of an act that could reasonably be foreseen rather than every single consequence that follows.

believe stem from Iran. Despite the increasing magnitude, at present these are more of a nuisance than a threat and the technique does not put sensitive information at risk. On the other hand, Chinese intrusions into DoD systems or Russian intrusions into SCADA systems would be extremely invasive. Professor Schmitt, however, cautions against applying this criterion too liberally because cyber exploitation is a ubiquitous tool of cyber espionage. He states, "Although highly invasive, espionage does not constitute a use of force (or armed attack) under international law absent a nonconsensual physical penetration of the target state's territory, as in the case of a warship or military aircraft which collects intelligence from within its territorial sea or airspace. Thus, actions such as disabling cyber security mechanisms to monitor keystrokes would, despite their invasiveness, be unlikely to be seen as a use of force."[23] Since it is virtually impossible to decide whether a cyber event is a prelude to an attack, an actual attack, a mere probe or espionage, until the ultimate event, how is this criterion useful at all today? Once again, one needs to wait-and-see the effect to make a proper determination. This means one will have to watch as an enemy pilfers information and exfiltrates it to know whether it is indeed espionage. Similarly, one will have to wait for an attack to begin before taking any response because one is unable to decide on a legally appropriate response without first knowing what *kind* of cyber event is playing out. By that point, it will be too late. On one hand, Professor Schmitt declares the intent of the adversary needs to be known before any action takes place. On the other, he states that disabling cyber security mechanisms to monitor keystrokes does not constitute a use of force. How does one know their intent in the latter scenario? The reality is that one does

---

[23] Schmitt, *supra* n. 7.

not unless the adversary announces their intent or one is already engaged in a declared armed conflict. Therefore, with cyber exploitation obfuscating our ability to make a determination, this criterion also offers little value in making such determinations.

The next criterion is measurability. It should go without saying that kinetic strikes are much more quantifiable and identifiable than the consequences of cyber operations. Kinetic strikes will likely result in damage or destruction to structures and to injury or death. Cyber consequences may not cause the same sort of easily recognizable results, yet they still produce the same ultimate effect as kinetic strikes. It may prove difficult, if not impossible, to measure, with any degree of accuracy, the subsequent consequences of a cyber event. Must one resort to trying to quantify the second and third order effects of a cyber event? Is it even possible to do so? Let us revisit the power-grid shutdown and examine the consequences thereof. A cyber event shuts down a power grid inside the United States, but causes no physical damage to any property. However, assume that it is sophisticated enough to merely act as a switch and simply turn off the power. The immediate effect is loss of power and is measurable by the number of people without power. The second and third order effects are much harder to measure. Perhaps physically weakened or elderly civilians die due to either lack of heat or lack of cooling, depending on the weather. Perhaps there is an increase in traffic fatalities due to lack of signaling lights. Maybe small children also die due to lack of operating medical services. Maybe looting occurs and property is damaged and people are injured. Can it be said that these are *direct* effects of the cyber event that can be quantified? This criterion is very similar to directness and the unforeseen victim discussion above. It is important to note that with the kinetic strike, causing the exact same result—loss of power—the focus is only on the direct effects, namely, the damage and destruction to property and injury or death to individuals. One would not necessarily look any further, because it is not needed. With cyber, one necessarily will be forced to do so, just to balance the criterion equation. Once again there is an inconsistency. On one hand equating cyber with kinetic events that cause the same effects and similar amounts of damage would result in similar measurability when applying the same rules and analysis. On the other hand, applying the same rules to cyber events that cause the overall same effects, but without necessarily creating the same measurable event yields different results. Treating cyber differently, on its own, may yield no measurable effects at all. Measurability, therefore, is not necessarily a good gauge, especially where the cyber event causes no actual physical harm or destruction.

The next criterion is presumptive legitimacy. This criterion, much like invasiveness, must be applied with caution. If you recall, acts which are not explicitly forbidden under international law are presumptively legitimate. This is true for propaganda, psychological warfare or, most importantly for cyber- espionage. Here one runs into the exact same problem as with invasiveness. Namely, it is virtually impossible to decide whether a cyber event is a prelude to an attack, an actual attack, a mere probe or espionage, until the ultimate event. Otherwise, one is left guessing and playing catch-up after the fact. In addition, today's cyber environment is populated with many non-state actor adversaries. Thus, presumptive legitimacy is not a good indicator for them because their acts are considered to be criminal. The problem, however, is determining the actor in the first place. Attribution plagues us once again. Even if the point of origin can be determined that is not definitive evidence of either state or non-state actor involvement. Unfortunately this is true even when the point of origin appears to be a government computer system. In the current cyber environment, presumptive legitimacy is only beneficial if one knows not only the intent of the actor up front but also the actor's identity. As discussed, knowing either is almost impossible in cyber, at least up front.

The final criterion is responsibility or, to be more precise, state responsibility. The more closely related an action is to a state, the more likely it will be seen as a use of force or armed attack. Professor Schmitt tells us that, "responsibility lies along a continuum from operations conducted by the state itself to those in which it is merely involved in some fashion."[24] While true, the practical utility of this standard in the current cyber environment is questionable. As discussed, it is very difficult to determine the intentions behind specific cyber events. Even if an event appears to be traceable to a specific country this is no guarantee that that country is responsible for or even condones the activity. However, international law allows some leeway, with regard to attribution. Professor Schmitt writes that, "So long as the victim-state has taken reasonable steps to identify the perpetrator of an armed attack, cyber or kinetic, and has drawn reasonable conclusions based on the results of those efforts, it may respond forcefully in self-defense."[25] In the rapidly evolving cyber landscape, a standard of care for reasonable efforts does not exist, and is unlikely to solidify in the foreseeable future. "That a state drew the wrong conclusion is of no direct relevance to the question of whether it acted lawfully in self-defense. Its responses are assessed as of the time it took

---

[24] *Id.*
[25] *Id.*

action, not ex post facto."[26] The assessment only has to be reasonable for the victim to take action against a cyber-intrusion that arises to either a use of force or armed attack. The difficult question is, even with this leeway, does existing technology support a "reasonable" determination? Although the ability to unmask one's adversaries is increasing, so is the ability of the adversaries to hide, spoof or cover their identity. Similarly, this criterion presents the same problems that presumptive legitimacy presents regarding unmasking the adversary.

To be fair, Professor Schmitt recognizes the limitations of his Analysis. He states: "The criteria are admittedly imprecise, thereby permitting states significant latitude in characterizing a cyber operation as a use of force, or not."[27] He has suggested that the factors are useful but not determinative, and they should not be applied mechanically. Rather, they need to be applied holistically according to the relevant context—that is, which factors are important and how they should be weighted will vary on a case-by-case basis. Moreover, the factors are not meant to be exhaustive, though they are often treated as such.[28] The framework is more useful for post hoc forensic analysis of particular cyber-attacks than for characterizing real-time operations.[29] He also writes that, "In light of the grave consequences that cyber operations can cause without physically harming persons or objects, this interpretation may seem wholly unsatisfactory. Nevertheless, it is the extant law."[30] Finally, he admits that, "The legal analysis ... should strike most readers as unsatisfactory.

---

[26] *Id.*
[27] *Id.*
[28] Schmitt, *supra*, n. 23.
[29] *Id.*
[30] Schmitt, *supra* n. 7.

Clear fault lines in the law governing the use of force have appeared because it is a body of law that predates the advent of cyber operations."[31]

In light of the above, the Schmitt analysis is still useful for states, but only to determine if an event that has already transpired met the threshold of use of force or armed attack. This has real value as it allows a state to go to the UN Security Council for proper action or take action on its own, i.e., self-defense. It can also justify countermeasures once a proper determination is made. However, if the response is too far removed from the actual event/intrusion, it may appear more like reprisal than a legitimate response. The Analysis is lacking, however, when considering current, on-going cyber operations. The problem is that current and on-going cyber operations are precisely what states and private industry are most concerned with characterizing today. His analysis was novel, groundbreaking and relevant at the time it was first proposed and for several years thereafter. As today's cyber realm has blossomed and moved to the forefront of our military, commercial and political lives, the relevance of this analysis is less clear.

In its day, the Schmitt Analysis worked and worked well. Ten years ago a cyber intrusion was rarely recognized until the effects manifested and alerted the victim. Using the Schmitt Analysis to determine whether those effects constituted a use of force or armed attack proved useful. Today, robust network defenses often discover such intrusions as they happen. The key now lies in making a Schmitt Analysis determination concurrent with the cyber intrusion. In the operational world this is referred to as law at the "speed of need." Moreover, today an intrusion is just as likely to originate with a non-state actor like Anonymous or Lulzsec or

---

[31] *Id.*

some other rogue or terrorist group. If true, then the Schmitt Analysis has no utility because it does not apply to non-state actors. Additionally, the vast majority of intrusions do not rise to the level of use of force or "armed" attack, but are exactly the events that our government and businesses deal with daily. While it may be true that the "black swan" or Pearl Harbor-like cyber event is worrisome, it has been reported that events of this magnitude have already been experienced, but in the context of cyber espionage rather than cyber-warfare. Thus, it is time for a new set of rules or an update of the Schmitt Analysis.

IV. TALLINN MANUAL

The Tallinn Manual consists of ninety-five rules meant to reflect customary international law as it applies to cyber. It was released by NATO's Cooperative Cyber Defense Centre of Excellence in March 21, 2013 and is the product of a three-year project. The rules were developed by an "International Group of Experts," including distinguished legal academics and practitioners, supported by a team of technical experts. USCYBERCOM, the International Committee of the Red Cross, and NATO each provided an observer.[32] Upon its release, the Manual caused quite a stir in the media and military channels. Despite its own admonitions not to use it as an authoritative document or settled law, many are in fact doing so.

Boiled down to its essence, the Manual answers a fundamental question; does international law apply to cyber activities? Not surprisingly, the answer is yes. Next the Tallinn authors attempted to dissect how international law applies to cyber. They discuss the customary, international rules, norms and laws applicable to traditional conflict as applied to cyber and

---

[32] See *supra* n.8.

make determinations regarding whether those rules, norms and laws are equally applicable when using cyber capabilities.

In answering the overarching question, the Tallinn Group looked at the International Court of Justice's Nuclear Weapons Advisory Opinion, where the Court considered whether the prohibition on the use of force governed the use of nuclear weapons.[33] The Court opined that the rules governing the use of force, "apply to any use of force, regardless of the weapons employed."[34] The Group concluded that since the rules apply to nuclear weapons, cyber is not so different and that the rules also apply to cyber. The Court also determined that international treaty and customary law that predated nuclear weapons governs their employment; thus so too with cyber. Finally, the Group considered the Martens Clause from the 1899 Hague Convention II, "[i]n cases not covered by this Protocol or by other international agreements, civilians and combatants remain under the protection and authority of the principles of international law derived from established custom, from the principles of humanity and from the dictates of public conscience."[35] Therefore, even in the absence of treaty law, humanitarian customs still apply. This is hardly controversial. In essence the Group seems to be restating well understood standards of state practice in the kinetic realm, and then restating the standards based on their understanding of what constitutes cyber. Indeed, Professor Schmitt reminds one that international law requires a legal review of

---

[33] Legality of the Threat or Use of Nuclear Weapons, 1996 I.C.J. 226 (May 14, 1993) (Advisory Opinion).
[34] *Id.*
[35] Protocol Additional (I) to the Geneva Conventions of 12 August 1949, and Relating to the Protection of Victims of International Armed Conflicts, June 8 1977, 1125 U.N.T.S. 3 (hereinafter Protocol 1).

weapons prior to fielding, "which *confirms the fact* that cyber weapons, as with other new weapons are subject to preexisting law."[36] (Emphasis added) To be sure, Air Force Instruction 51-402, implements international law and mandates such a review.[37]

The introduction to the Manual describes and delineates what it does and does not do. It spells out, with great particularity, its application and non-application to certain areas of law and conflict. Of note, the Group limits their discussion to use of force and armed conflict. Cyber activities that do not rise to the level of either, which includes espionage, are not discussed. The Group focused on cyber-to-cyber operations, excluding kinetic-to-cyber operations and likewise excluding traditional electronic warfare attacks, like jamming.[38] Their rationale for excluding discussion on those topics is that they are already well understood under the law of armed conflict. This ignores the overlap and fusion of electronic warfare and cyber warfare capabilities, an issue of great interest within the military Services.

The Manual is additionally divided into two major parts, Part A and Part B. Part A discusses International Cyber Security Law and Part B discusses The Law of Cyber Armed Conflict. The parts are broken down into chapters and sections and each section encompasses the rules, discussing the details and answering the pertinent questions to arrive at the 95

---

[36] Schmitt, *International Law in Cyberspace: The Koh Speech and Tallinn Manual Juxtaposed*, 54 HARV. INT'L L.J. ONLINE 13 (2012), *available at:* http://www.harvardilj.org/2012/12/online-articles-online_54_schmitt/.

[37] Secretary of the Air Force, Air Force Instruction 51-402, Legal Reviews of Weapons and Cyber Capabilities (July 27, 2011), *available at:* http://www.fas.org/irp/doddir/usaf/afi51-402.pdf.

[38] See *supra* n.8.

rules. For instance, Chapter One discusses states and cyberspace, including sovereignty, jurisdiction and state responsibility. Chapter Two discusses the use of force, including its prohibition and self-defense. Chapter Three, under Part B, discusses the law of armed conflict generally. Chapter Four discusses the conduct of hostilities, focusing on attacks. Chapter Five discusses certain persons, objects, and activities, including medical, religious, detained, children and cultural property, the natural environment and collective punishment. Chapter Six discusses occupation and Chapter Seven discusses neutrality.[39]

Let's look at some of the rules as enumerated and explained by the Group. Following that, exploring them in the context of whether they offer anything new and substantive or whether they merely restate current practice.

Rule one reads, "A state may exercise control over cyber infrastructure and activities within its sovereign territory."[40] The experts agreed that, "although no State may claim sovereignty over cyberspace per se, States may exercise sovereign prerogatives over any cyber infrastructure located on their territory, as well as activities associated with that cyber infrastructure."[41] Likewise, the experts declared that, "it is the sovereignty that a State enjoys over territory that gives it the right to control cyber infrastructure and cyber activities within its territory. Accordingly, cyber infrastructure situated in the land territory, internal waters, territorial sea (including its bed and subsoil), archipelagic waters, or national airspace is subject to the sovereignty of the territorial state."[42]

---

[39] *Id.*
[40] *Id.*
[41] *Id.*
[42] *Id.*

While it is true that no state exercises control over cyberspace it makes perfect sense to declare a state exercises control over those things within its sovereign territory. This revelation is not surprising. Certainly states exercise control over all infrastructure within their sovereign territory, whether government owned or privately owned. For instance, the government regulates dams, power plants, buildings, roads, telephony, etc. and, has been doing so for many years. In this context there is little difference between normal, old-fashioned infrastructure and cyber infrastructure. Both are composed of physical components residing within sovereign territory. Likewise traditional activities that occur within the sovereign territory of a state have been controlled or regulated for many, many years. Cyber activities occurring within the sovereign territory of a state are not sufficiently different from traditional kinetic activities that different rules should apply. Phone and other wire communications are a classic example of "traditional" activities that have been controlled and/or regulated by states. Cyber is a variation on the same theme. Smart-phones are a prime example of both old and new technologies converging in one device. Both technologies, however, are regulated and controlled. Therefore, it stands to reason that the same rules would apply to cyber activities and infrastructure as for traditional activities and infrastructure. The most that this rule provides is, perhaps, definitional granularity between cyberspace itself and cyber infrastructure.

Rule two provides, "Without prejudice to applicable international obligations, a State may exercise its jurisdiction: (a) over persons engaged in cyber activities on its territory; (b) over cyber infrastructure located on its territory; and (c) Extraterritorially, in accordance with international law."[43] Jurisdiction

---

[43] *Id.*

encompasses the authority to prescribe, enforce, and adjudicate. It extends to all matters, including those that are civil, criminal, or administrative in nature. From a legal perspective, jurisdiction is determined by physical or legal presence of a person or object within the sovereign territory. This is known as either in personam or in rem jurisdiction. In other words, a state can exercise jurisdiction over the activities of persons located within the state and also over objects within its territory.

      This is long established state practice. Several U.S. laws, namely the Computer Fraud and Abuse Act and the Electronic Communications Privacy Act, have resolved many of these tricky jurisdictional issues long ago. Moreover, aspects of copyright and patent law have also answered some, if not all, of these types of jurisdictional questions. Attribution in the cyber realm makes it difficult to determine, with legal accuracy, who or what is behind a cyber event. In some cases, it is even difficult to determine the origin of the event. Even so, attribution is more of a technical issue than a legal one. Besides, as our technology has evolved, the existing laws mentioned above have maintained their applicability regardless of the difficulty in applying them. This rule simply expands on rule one—if a state has control over certain things, people and objects, then legally, it should also have jurisdiction over them. It should not surprise anyone that a state exercises jurisdiction over persons engaged in non-cyber activities within its territory or jurisdiction over non-cyber infrastructure. Why then would a state not also have jurisdiction over persons engaging in cyber activities within its territory or over the cyber infrastructure being utilized? Indeed, the examples mentioned above prove that the United States has been doing just that.

Rule nine states, "[A] State injured by an internationally wrongful act may resort to proportionate countermeasures, including cyber countermeasures, against the responsible state."[44] Some of these terms require definitions to fully understand stated rule. "Countermeasures are necessary and proportionate actions that a 'victim-State' takes in response to a violation of international law by an 'offending State' to induce compliance with international law by the offending State."[45] An internationally wrongful act occurs when, "conduct consisting of an act or omission: (a) is either attributable to a state under international law; and (b) constitutes a breach of an international obligation of the state."[46]

Rule nine adds cyber to an accepted definition. States have always been authorized to resort to countermeasures. Now they may do so using cyber countermeasures. It is helpful to think of cyber as one of many tools in a toolbox of national power that sovereign states have at their disposal. Under international law, states have an obligation to ensure weapons they anticipate using are lawful. Though internal mechanisms for ensuring compliance can vary, in general once a weapon has been reviewed for compliance with the Law of Armed Conflict ("LOAC"), and its use is found to be lawful, it may be added to a nation's arsenal. Likewise, once a cyber capability has

---

[44] See The Tallinn Manual, *supra* n. 8.
[45] *Id*.
[46] Draft Articles on Responsibility of States for Internationally Wrongful Acts, pt. 2, Arts. 28–41, in Report of the International Law Commission on the Work of Its Fifty-third Session, UN GAOR, 56th Sess., Supp. No. 10, at 43, UN Doc. A/56/10 (2001), *available at:* http://untreaty.un.org/ilc/texts/instruments/english/commentaries/9_6_2001.pdf, reprinted in JAMES CRAWFORD, THE INTERNATIONAL LAW COMMISSION'S ARTICLES ON STATE RESPONSIBILITY: INTRODUCTION, TEXT AND COMMENTARIES (2002).

been reviewed for compliance with the LOAC, and found to be in compliance, it also may be provided to operational units for use. The LOAC review is not a substitute for a subsequent review of the contemplated use of a weapon in a specific operation; however it is a necessary predicate safeguard. Granted, countermeasures are not the same thing as responses to either a use of force or armed attack. Cyber-countermeasures are, nonetheless, tools that remain an available option. It would make little or no sense to allow states to use cyber in response to use of force and armed attacks, but to limit the tools available for lesser offenses.

Rule twenty states, "[c]yber operations executed in the context of an armed conflict are subject to the LOAC."[47] This, however, begs the question, when *aren't* cyber operations subject to LOAC? The most obvious and relevant answer is, when the operation is conducted as espionage.

Cyber-capabilities are tools to be used by military commanders just like any other tool or weapon they would use. New cyber capabilities undergo a capabilities review, just like kinetic weapons do. Therefore, it stands to reason that the same rules apply to cyber capabilities as to traditional kinetic weapons. To be certain, US commanders and their allies have been doing so for many years now. It is particularly noteworthy that the Tallinn Group specifically excluded discussing traditional electronic warfare like jamming because those rules are already well established. Cyber is not so different from those "traditional" methods and means that the rules would somehow be different or inapplicable. It is fair to suggest that cyber warfare is closely related to, and may have grown from electronic warfare. Cyber is much broader and encompasses many

---

[47] See The Tallinn Manual, *supra* n. 8.

more activities, but the underlying character of the activities is the same. It is accepted that, *any* operation executed in the context of an armed conflict is subject to the LOAC. It makes no difference what it is called or how it is defined. States cannot evade their duties and obligations under the LOAC by calling their operations by another name. It is DoD policy that, "[m]embers of the DoD Components comply with the law of war during all armed conflicts, however such conflicts are characterized, and in all other military operations."[48] It should be noted that this is not new policy, merely the restatement of long-standing US policy.

Rule thirty defines cyber-attack as, "a cyber operation, whether offensive or defensive that is reasonably expected to cause injury or death to persons or damage or destruction to objects."[49] It is generally understood that the focus, in defining an attack under the law of armed conflict, is whether the act produces violent consequences. Namely, whether any property was damaged or destroyed or whether individuals were harmed or killed. Therefore, it is not the act itself, but rather the subsequent consequences thereof that matters. The problem is that this rule fails to address the value of intangible property in a networked world. If a cyber operation prevents fuel from being delivered to aircraft and the aircraft are thus unable to complete a kinetic operation, is this an "attack." It would seem so, though no injury, death, damage or destruction of objects occurred.

Thus, the Tallinn definition of cyber-attack is no more than the definition of attack with cyber tacked-on. It fails to address the central issue raised by the new

---

[48] Directive No. 2311.01E: DoD Law of War Program, U.S. DEP'T DEF. 2 (May 9, 2006), *available at*: http://www.dtic.mil/whs/directives/corres/pdf/231101e.pdf.
[49] See The Tallinn Manual, *supra* n. 8.

technical context. Of course, if one labels something as an attack, it must meet the definition of one. For instance, one could define a school as a building or other structure wherein people meet and are taught various subjects in a learning environment. To define a girls-school, one would simply state the same thing, but merely tack-on "girls'. Thus, a cyber-attack and a traditional kinetic attack are essentially the same thing, creating the same violent consequences. It is merely the manner in which they are initiated that differs. Although this rule states the obvious, it does create a situation where a cyber event and a kinetic event can be labeled different things even though they bring about the exact same result. A cyber event that shuts down a power grid may do so without causing any harm or damage at all, whereas a kinetic event, causing the same thing certainly causes damage and destruction. One would be an attack, but the other would not under this rule.

Rule forty-nine explains that, "[c]yber-attacks that are not directed at a lawful target, and consequently are of a nature to strike lawful targets and civilians or civilian objects without distinction, are prohibited."[50]

Once again the Tallinn Group merely substitute "cyber-attack" for traditional "kinetic" attack to reach a commonsense conclusion. Furthermore, US military commanders and their allies have been complying with this rule for some number of years now. Lawyers are embedded with operational and tactical units, carrying out attacks, to specifically provide legal advice regarding distinction. To be sure, international law requires that lawyers be available to offer such advice. Additional Protocol I (API) to the Geneva Convention states, "The High Contracting Parties at all times, and the Parties to the conflict in time of armed conflict, shall ensure that legal advisers are available, when necessary, to advise

---

[50] *Id.*

military commanders at the appropriate level on the application of the Conventions and this Protocol and on the appropriate instruction to be given to the armed forces on this subject."[51] Even though the United States has not ratified API, US rules also dictate that commanders have legal advice. Chairman of the Joint Chiefs of Staff Instruction (CJCSI) 5810.01D, directs Combatant Commanders to, among other things, "Integrate legal advisers into planning sessions and conferences for military operations and exercises to enable them to provide advice concerning domestic and international law, including the law of war, compliance."[52] In other words, this rule informs that the traditional, core principles of the law of war; namely, distinction, apply to cyber-attacks as they do for any attack. Cyber certainly predates the Tallinn Manual and cyber capabilities used in and during war also predates the Tallinn Manual. Nonetheless, US commanders and allies have been abiding by the LOAC even when using cyber tools to create kinetic-like effects. Indeed, the Tallinn Group has noted in Rule twenty that LOAC applies to cyber. Rule forty-nine then, is simply providing more, unneeded details, namely noting the principle of distinction is also applicable to cyber.

Rule ninety-one declares that, "The exercise of belligerent rights by cyber means directed against neutral cyber infrastructure is prohibited."[53] In other words, one can't deliberately target cyber infrastructure in a neutral state/territory or within the control of a neutral state, if also within neutral territory.

---

[51] Protocol I, *supra* n. 35.
[52] CHAIRMAN, JOINT CHEIFS OF STAFF INSTR. 5810.1D, IMPLEMENTATION OF THE DOD LAW OF WAR PROGRAM (30 April 2010) at para. 6f(2).
[53] See The Tallinn Manual, *supra* n. 8.

This is a well-established rule, customary in nature, in the kinetic realm. Its application, therefore, in the cyber realm is not startling. Indeed, it is wholly expected. Moreover, US and their allies have been in compliance for many years. Once again, this coincides with the principle of distinction. US commanders have been complying with the principles of the law of war for every tool they use, including cyber capabilities. To be sure, the use of cyber capabilities is so constrained, due to these issues and concerns, that the approval authority for their use is incredibly high.

Using the Tallinn manual one must consider equating cyber intrusions with kinetic strikes, amounting to use of force or armed attack. Thus, using the same rules for both seems to work. However, as has been demonstrated above, all cyber intrusions are not the same as kinetic strikes and therefore, the same rules cannot apply to both equally. Focusing on cyber intrusions falling below use of force precludes the application of the rules applicable to kinetic strikes.

Despite being over 250 pages and taking approximately three years to complete, the Manual really offers little new or surprising. It is an exercise of academic debate, essentially restating what has been practice for some time by the United States, but failing to address the central issues raised by the emerging technical landscape. The Manual "codifies" that practice by substituting-in the term cyber. Achieving international law for cyber is a complex challenge and will take many nations agreeing over a substantial period of years. The Manual would better serve practitioners by listing and discussing those rules which the Group could not reach a consensus. This is the work which needs to be done by the international law community in order to address the emerging cyber landscape. These are the questions that remain to be answered as technology increases and cyber becomes even more conventional and widespread. The Manual's usefulness lies with the discussion of the rules and the rational. It allows legal advisors and practitioners to engage in spirited debate in those areas where the Group could not agree. This will help guide future debates and help answer some of the harder questions.

V. U.S. POLICY

Current US cyber policy, concerning cyber intrusions, cyber defense, and cyber offense, can generally be divided between Joint Publication (JP) 3-12 and Presidential Policy Directive (PPD) 20. PPD 20 is more of a whole-of-government approach while JP 3-12 is focused on DoD. Combining both produces a general overview of current US cyber policy. A few unclassified terms will be discussed that are solely those within JP 3-12. No discussion of PPD 20 will occur to avoid potential security issues. I do not mean to suggest that these two documents are the only ones providing guidance on US cyber policy. That is certainly not the case. Rather, they focus more on the relevant issues discussed throughout this paper and provide a means to compare and contrast.

First the list of unclassified definitions will be identified. A discussion on whether those definitions are helpful or whether they hinder our understanding of cyber will follow. Finally there is a review on clear distinctions and some contradictions between the terms used and others previously discussed.

Countermeasures:

> That form of military science that, by the employment of devices and/or techniques, has as its objective the impairment of the operational effectiveness of enemy activity. In

cyberspace, countermeasures are intended to identify the source of a threat to the Department of Defense information networks and use nonintrusive techniques to stop or mitigate offensive activity in cyberspace. Countermeasures are a subset of defensive cyberspace operations response actions.[54]

Cyberspace: "A global domain within the information environment consisting of the interdependent networks of information technology infrastructures and resident data, including the Internet, telecommunication networks, computer systems, and embedded processors and controllers."[55]

Cyberspace attack: "Cyberspace actions that create various direct denial effects in cyberspace (i.e., degradation, disruption, or destruction) and manipulation that leads to denial that is hidden or that manifests in the physical domains."[56]

Cyberspace intelligence, surveillance, and reconnaissance: "Activities conducted in cyberspace that synchronize and integrate the planning and operation of sensors, assets, and processing, exploitation, and dissemination systems in direct support of current and future operations."[57]

Cyberspace defense: "Actions normally created within Department of Defense cyberspace for securing, operating, and defending the Department of Defense

---

[54] Joint Chiefs of Staff, Joint Cyberspace Publication (Joint Publication JP 3-12) (July 5, 2010), *incorporating change 1* (Nov. 30, 2011) (hereinafter JP 3-12).
[55] *Id.*
[56] *Id.*
[57] *Id.*

information networks. Specific actions include protect, detect, characterize, counter, and mitigate."[58]

Cyberspace operations as: "The employment of cyberspace capabilities where the primary purpose is to achieve objectives in or through cyberspace."[59]

Defensive cyberspace operations as: "Passive and active cyberspace operations intended to preserve the ability to utilize friendly cyberspace capabilities and protect data, networks, net centric capabilities, and other designated systems." It defines defensive cyberspace operations response action as, "Deliberate, authorized defensive measures or activities taken outside of the defended network to protect and defend Department of Defense cyberspace capabilities or other designated systems."[60]

Offensive cyberspace operations: "Cyberspace operations intended to project power by the application of force in or through cyberspace."[61]

It is reasonable to suggest that the definitions above are not very helpful for practitioners. It is a fair assessment to suggest that some of them are detrimental to what the overarching policy should be. Some hinder one's actions by defining too broadly, while others don't go far enough. Moreover, there appear to be some internal inconsistencies as well.

For instance, let's look at the definition of countermeasures again. Countermeasures seek to impair the operational effectiveness of enemy activity. At first blush that sounds suspiciously like disruption or manipulation, which would qualify as an attack too. The second part informs one that countermeasures use nonintrusive techniques to stop or mitigate offensive

---

[58] *Id.*
[59] *Id.*
[60] JP 3-12, *supra* n. 54.
[61] *Id.*

activity in cyberspace. Now it appears that the definition contradicts itself. On one hand, impairment seems to require some positive action against the enemy—impairment. Indeed, countermeasures go beyond the perimeter of the network. On the other hand, nonintrusive seems to indicate just the opposite. Unfortunately, nonintrusive is not further defined anywhere nor is impair. Finally, it has been noted that the countermeasures are a subset of defensive cyberspace operations response actions. Response actions again infer taking some action outside one's own networks, presumably nonintrusive—whatever that means. Without clear definitions of all pertinent terms, one is left with nothing more than a circular definition that confuses more than it clarifies.

Next consider cyber-attack and cyber effects together, because one is informed that the attack creates the effects. First, the definition states that an attack creates various effects and then several examples are provided. However, the definition does not tell one whether those listed effects are the only effects allowed or whether more exist. To remedy that, one needs an additional definition specifically defining those effects as manipulation, disruption, denial, degradation, or destruction. Ostensibly, this tells one that the list is all inclusive. It is also known that those items are incredibly broad, meaning that almost anything in cyber could constitute an attack by this definition. However, the second part articulates that the denial must either be hidden or manifest itself in the physical domain. So, despite the apparent broadness of the first part, the second part provides limitation. This limitation, further defining an attack, can be used to claim an action is *not* an attack. For instance, one can advise their commander that she may take an action that is not hidden or will not manifest itself in the physical domain and it is therefore not an attack. Therefore, the approval authority for taking such an action may be a lot lower, allowing greater leeway. Now, perhaps one deliberately placed this "loophole" into the definition to allow for flexibility. Or, perhaps it was an oversight. In either case a "loophole" exists.

Lastly, consider offensive cyberspace operations. The definition is short so simply restated here: Cyberspace operations intended to project power by the application of force in or through cyberspace. Once again descriptive terms are not further defined. What, exactly does "project power" mean? What is an "application of force?" Even if force was defined it would not mean much outside of DoD channels. Use of force in international law is not completely settled even regarding kinetic strikes. Use of force in the cyber context is much more difficult to discern and certainly not settled. The US definition, however, seems to imply that any offensive action the US takes would necessarily include some use of force. So, the US makes it easy on their enemies by declaring what is being done is a use of force and difficult on itself for the very same reason. Moreover, there is an apparent disconnect between the definition of cyber-attack and offensive cyberspace operation. One would think that all attacks would be offensive and that all offensive cyberspace operations would be an attack. That, however, is not the case. An offensive cyberspace operation, that is either not hidden or does not manifest in the physical domain, would not be considered a cyber-attack. A cyber-attack that does not rise to the level of application of force would not be considered an offensive cyberspace operation.

Finally, compare some of the US policy definitions with those of the Tallinn manual and Professor Schmitt. Bear in mind that the rules developed by the Tallinn Group presumably reflects consensus as to the applicable law currently governing cyber conflict. In other words, the rules do not reflect best practice or preferred policy, but the law as it currently stands.[62] Note the fact that so many differences and discrepancies exist. If there is general agreement, at least from the Tallinn Group, on the law as it currently stands, then why do the views cited seem so divergent?

The US policy definition of cyber-attack is not clear or concise. It does, however, broadly include those things not normally associated with a traditional understanding of kinetic attack—manipulation, disruption, denial, degradation, or destruction. This is especially true if one tries to equate cyber-attack with kinetic attack. The Manual definition makes clear that a cyber-attack is an act of violence either against a person or object and that the focus is on the consequences and not the initiating act itself. Thus, the consequences of a cyber-attack must generate some violence to some person or thing. Notably, the Manual definition includes attacks on data if the consequences manifest as violence against either a person or thing. Moreover, the Manual also indicates that interference with functionality of a physical thing constitutes an attack, *if* restoration of the functionality requires replacement of physical components. This is perhaps where the two definitions diverge greatly. The US policy definition only requires manipulation or disruption, which presumably applies to data; in other words, if one limits the scope of an operation to affecting data that is a cyber-attack. Clearly this is not the case under the Manual definition because there is no violent consequence to either people or things.

Comparing the Schmitt analysis to both the Manual and US policy definition adds to the confusion. Professor Schmitt focuses on harm to people or things,

---

[62] See The Tallinn Manual, *supra* n. 8.

which is in line with the Manual's focus on violent consequences. However, Professor Schmitt's criterion of severity is a sliding scale—the more severe the consequences the more likely it is a use of force. So it appears there are three separate and distinct definitions when use of a cyber capability would constitute an attack. US policy only requires manipulation or disruption of data. The Manual requires some physical manifestation of the consequences and Professor Schmitt requires some level of severity based on scale, scope, and duration. Thus, it is possible to arrive at separate and contradictory answers of whether an event constitutes an attack. Changing data to reflect something different to the observer than what is actually there would be an attack under US policy (manipulating data), but clearly would not under both the Manual and Schmitt analysis (no physical manifestation and no harm).

An additional discrepancy arises when considering the introduction of malware into an adversary system. The Manual suggests that, "the introduction of malware or production-level defects that are either time-delayed or activate on the occurrence of a particular event is an attack."[63] Professor Schmitt, however, states that, "the introduction into a state's cyber systems of vulnerabilities that are capable of destructive activation at some later date would not constitute a threat of the use of force unless their presence is known to the target state and the originating state exploits them for some coercive purpose."[64] US policy tends to align with the Manual, but for a different reason—insertion into an adversary system would likely constitute manipulation. Thus, it isn't difficult to imagine a scenario where insertion of malware or

---

[63] *Id.*
[64] Schmitt, *supra* n. 23.

vulnerabilities into an adversary's system would yield different answers depending on which definition one chooses to use.

Thus, current US cyber policy is based on terms that are not well defined and, the meaning of the terms is not consistent with the extant law as defined by the Tallinn Group. Some of the terms contradict others and some add layers of unnecessary constraint. Based on this context it is clear that US cyber policy is definitely not moving in the right direction. Instead of taking the lead and crafting a bold and workable cyber policy, the United States is instead immersed in wordsmithing in an apparent attempt to appear as if they are doing something while really accomplishing nothing substantive. This confusion over terms is even evident in the media, which compounds the problem, not only for us, but also for our allies and even our adversaries. For instance, a recent article in the Washington Post indicates that, "China on Wednesday again denied that it has used cyberattacks to steal U.S. military and business secrets, after new accusations were leveled in May 2013."[65] Of course China is not using *cyber-attacks* to steal information. They are engaging in cyber-espionage to steal. Undoubtedly there is a misunderstanding between cyber-attack, cyber-espionage and cyber-crime which only contributes to the problem and sows confusion.

VI. CONCLUSION

It is clear that our adversary's growing cyber capabilities are a real and continuing threat to the United States and indeed, the world. Without meaningful, useful concepts, definitions, rules, policy and law there will continue to be a struggle in a vain search for

---

[65] William Wan, *China Again Rejects Hacking Allegation*, WASH. POST, at 7, May 30, 2013.

consensus. Despite the attempts discussed in this article, the legal community has not achieved anything even approaching accord. One cannot be so naïve to believe that all nations will agree, but hopeful that if just a handful of influential nations could at least agree on some basic and fundamental concepts, definitions, rules, policy and law, then the rest may follow suit. It may be argued that the Tallinn Manual did just that. Presumably the NATO nations agreed with the rules delineated in the Manual—several key nations. However, as this article points out, those rules are not necessarily in line with either US policy or respected cyber intellectuals like Professor Schmitt and certainly not with other non-NATO nations like China or Russia.

If we continue down this path, issuing a hodge-podge of cyber concepts, definitions, rules, policy and law, an international law of cyber warfare will not develop. Instead, additional cyber intrusions are only getting worse and becoming more dangerous. Likewise, if the U.S. continues to hamper itself with convoluted and, sometimes contradictory concepts, definitions, rules, policy and law, it will fail to take the lead in this field and risk becoming irrelevant. Emerging and re-emerging powers may take charge. Countries like China or Russia or India or Brazil may prove to be the leaders in this area, and most assuredly they will not have the United States best interests at heart.

Without doubt the United States has the potential to lay the groundwork for a workable international legal structure. Professor Schmitt has already contributed significantly, but it is time to build on his early work in the field. The Tallinn Group has also contributed to global understanding as well. Likewise, their contributions must also be further developed. The United States and NATO can't simply dictate to the rest of the world. It has been hinted that

Russia plans to develop its own "anti-Tallinn" manual. If true, then a separate coalition will from around Russia. Two competing groups of cyber concepts, definitions, rules, policy and laws will then exist. At that point, it will almost be impossible for customary international cyber law to develop. Others with diverse views and opinions must be included, if we ever hope to develop the cyber arena in a meaningful way. At the very least, the definitions should align and be consistent with rules. The rules should align with the policy. The policy should align with broad concepts. Concepts should align with the law. Unless and until this is addressed, one cannot expect any consensus either.

Is Cyber Espionage a Form of Market Manipulation

By Noah Bledstein*

On March 3rd 2013 the New York Times ran the article "As Hacking Against U.S. Rises, Experts Try to Pin Down Motive".[1] The thrust of the article is that industry and government agencies have proof the Chinese are engaged in great deal of cyber espionage against American companies, but experts are having a hard time ascribing specific motives to many of the "attacks".

The Chinese motives certainly aren't limited to a single purpose. There seems little doubt that they steal intellectual property for its intrinsic value in making sophisticated products without incurring the expense of research and development. It has also been reported that they target sensitive corporate strategies in order to provide Chinese companies an upper hand when negotiating with foreign competitors. Why wouldn't

---

* Noah Bledstein recently retired from his position as the Chief of Cyber Law, 24th Air Force, Lackland Air Force Base, TX. 24th Air Force provides combat-ready forces trained and equipped to conduct sustained cyber operations, fully integrated with air and space operations. Maj. (Ret.) Bledstein specializes in military cyber law, information operations law, intelligence oversight law, telecommunications law and the law of emerging technologies. From 2006-2009 he was the Chief of Cyber Law for Eighth Air Force JA where his clients included AFCYBER(P), the Air Force Partnership with Industry cyber defense initiative, the Cyber Division of the Global Strike Air Operations Center and the Air Force Information Operations Center.

[1] Perlroth, Sanger, and Schmidt, *As Hacking Against U.S. Rises, Experts Try to Pin Down Motive*, NEW YORK TIMES (March 3, 2013).

they? China does not draw a line between commerce and government, quite the opposite. However the article also points out that China is too heavily invested in the U.S. economy to want to hurt it.

The New York Times article pulls together two important factors without raising what, in retrospect, seems an obvious question; is a significant motive for Chinese cyber espionage the manipulation of U.S. stock and commodities markets through the use of illegally obtained "insider" information. Stated another way, is it possible to correlate the buying and selling of U.S. securities with intrusions into the companies which are being bought and sold? Does the SEC have access to the information about attacks on companies that would allow it to initiate enforcement actions to deter this sort of market manipulation?

A spate of recent news articles and public protests about the breadth and commercial focus of Chinese espionage appears to be the first real move toward public diplomacy as a means of addressing network espionage. These activities are often described using the language of warfare, however from a legal perspective the activities fall squarely within traditional espionage. This public discussion is a significant first step toward establishing international norms which are a pre-condition for the development of customary international law. Ironically, development of a body of customary international law of cyber warfare may have little substantive effect on this form of economic warfare.

It should be noted that this move toward openness was suggested in the Hathaway cyber report to the 44th President five years ago.[2] With regard to cyber

---

[2] Securing Cyberspace for the 44th Presidency A Report of the CSIS Commission on Cybersecurity for the 44th Presidency, Committee for Strategic and International Studies, December 2008.

warfare, standards clearly need to be established, however, an international legal standard for espionage already exists. Stated in laymen's terms the standards are: do onto others better than they are doing onto you, deny everything when caught and don't get caught in a way that allows the victim to exercise their jurisdiction over your people or assets. Espionage is legal under international law, but generally illegal under the laws of the country in which the spying is occurring. To restate the obvious, human intelligence operations require spies on the ground that can be caught, jailed, traded or executed. For our adversaries, cyber espionage has the great advantage that if and when the victims catch the hackers, the main consequences are the loss of access into the targeted systems and the loss of the use of the programs used to find and extract useful information from the targeted networks. Even these consequences assume that the victims have the resources and sophistication to close the "back doors" which allowed the hackers in and patch their systems to prevent the same malware from being used against their systems again. This doesn't provide the victims with much leverage.

Imprecise use of language is a substantive problem in this arena. Where cyber espionage is concerned the term "attack" is invariably misused. The vast majority of cyber espionage is more analogous to theft than physical assault. It is being widely reported that U.S. and other western corporate networks are probed, breached and mined for sensitive data on a regular basis. These activities can easily be characterized as theft and espionage, but most fall well short of rising to a level where they can be regarded as a use of force or act of war.

From a political and military perspective, particularly when the question is whether to consider the use of kinetic or cyber responses to dissuade such hacking, it is only when activities are directly malicious, attributable to identifiable hostile forces and causing damage which is measurable that such activities can be accurately characterized as an "attack". There is no bright line standard for what constitutes an "attack" in international law. Cyber "attacks" can include a spectrum of activities; some examples might be seeding a network with the electronic equivalent of time bombs for use during a conflict or modifying the substance of information on the network to make it unreliable.

As in the "real" or kinetic world, how a nation responds to a cyber-attack is always based on the relative value of the damage to the people, property or principles of the victim.[3] The semantic problem when describing cyber conflict is that sloppy use of language causes confusion between warfare, criminal activity and nation state espionage. Whether intentional or not, this has caused a lack of clarity about the legal character of the activities in question and has caused confusion about exactly who in government or industry should receive the authority and funding to respond. How government or industry can respond is equally unclear.

It is important to note that even if clear rules for the military use of force in cyberspace or the conduct of "cyber war" existed, it would be of little help in this commercial context.

Practical problems require actionable solutions. This is what makes the possibility that Chinese actors are engaging in market manipulation so intriguing. Unlike other forms of cyber conflict, blatant stock manipulation by a major economic power could have tangible legal consequences inside the United States. All cyber activities leave records which, with enough

---

[3] Schmitt, *Cyberspace and International Law: The Penumbral Mist of Uncertainty*, 126 HARV. L. REV. F. 176 (2013).

diligence, resources and effort, can be used as evidence. If the Securities and Exchange Commission or State's Attorney Generals are presented with forensically acceptable evidence of illegal market manipulation, either could initiate enforcement actions that would put Chinese or other threat actor's assets at risk. Civil forfeiture of assets connected to drug crimes has proved an effective tool for law enforcement. It seems likely that the dollar value of the property in question dwarfs that seized in drug cases.

To date treating espionage as a form of economic crime which can cause the perpetrator's property to be placed at risk does not appear to be a response that has been seriously considered. It could be that the United States government, the states and industry need to reconsider how to deal with this rapidly growing problem. What is really meant when our leaders talk about bringing "all aspects of national power" to the fight? In the age of "big data", it seems reasonable to suggest that the government can cooperate with industry to conduct research to correlate the cyber "attacks," more accurately described as espionage campaigns, with existing records of stock and commodities market transactions.

In light of corporate resistance to revealing hacks of their networks, this sort of effort will require legislation to clarify when Sarbanes Oxley reporting of such incidents is required as well as limitations of potential liability associated with such reporting. By collecting the right data and developing targeted analytic tools, law enforcement and intelligence organizations could look for hacking trends that appear related to subsequent market activity. Once alerted to the possibility of specific crimes they could "drill down" through the data to determine whether company logs provide enough evidence to support an investigation by the Securities and Exchange Commission or a state attorney general. This could lead to exactly the same sort of enforcement actions which currently attempts to keep American companies and powerful economic actors honest.

What has been described as a "cyber war" may be a new form of economic warfare. More likely, targeted economic espionage is just one manifestation of the aggressive type of international and domestic capitalism that the Chinese view as the new normal.[4] Regardless of how it is ultimately defined, this motive for nation state sponsored hacking of American companies is worth examination. It provides a rational explanation for some of the economic espionage China appears to have engaged in. This may not be a form of warfare or conflict our military, intelligence or financial regulatory communities are currently authorized, funded, equipped or trained to address, but reality dictates that we engage in the fight we find ourselves in.

If new technologies are allowing our adversaries to change the nature of warfare, it is time to use existing legal mechanisms to address this behavior. Diplomacy and warfare are ultimately about holding that which our adversaries value at risk. Continuing to accept the status quo is not an acceptable option. A broader understanding and more aggressive engagement in the current cyber conflict through new uses of information and analytic tools in concert with enabling legislation and aggressive enforcement of existing domestic laws is overdue.

---

[4] Wong, *Hackers Find China New Land of Opportunity*, NEW YORK TIMES (May 22, 2013).

www.ingramcontent.com/pod-product-compliance
Lightning Source LLC
Chambersburg PA
CBHW080932170526
45158CB00008B/2260